CW00485722

The
Folk House
Anthology
edited by
Rosemary Dun
and
Kate Gardiner

First published in 2007
by City Chameleon
P.O. Box 2354, Bristol, BS6 9ZN
www.citychameleon.co.uk

Cover designed by Chris Pink, 2007
Photo © Chris Pink, 2007

Anthology copyright © The Folk House, 2007
Copyright for each piece lies with individual authors © 2007
Foreward copyright © Lucy English, 2007

This book is sold subject to the condition that it shall not, by way of trade or otherwise, be lent, resold, hired out or otherwise circulated without the publisher's prior consent in any form of binding or cover other than that in which it is published and without a similar condition including this condition being imposed on the subsequent purchaser.

The publication of this book was made possible thanks to a grant from Arts Council England.

ISBN 978-0-9551180-2-9

CONTENTS

To our students, past and present,
and all at The Folk House.

Foreword

"Creativity" is a buzz word much mentioned in the field of education. One of the purposes of education, theorists enthuse, is to foster creativity in children. What they have forgotten, and is easy for all of us to forget, is that all humans are creative. We are born with a natural ability to create. Young children paint, draw, dance, dress up, pretend to fly, pretend to be fairies, pretend to be monsters, make things out of boxes, make up stories, and live in a world filled with creativity. Unfortunately it is often education that erases this out of us.

Twenty years ago I went to a creative writing course at the Folk House run by the talented writer Geraldine Kay. I had some vague idea I wanted to write. I had some vague memory of making up stories as a child. I had some notion that my current life had become a series of repetitive tasks and I wanted 'something else'.

I am glad I made that journey. Writing is now an integral part of my life and my own creativity is fostered on a daily basis. It is as essential to me as breathing. All the people in this anthology have discovered this too. Creativity is not reserved for a few select individuals, it is an inheritance belonging to us all.

When you read this anthology remember that these men and women are people like you. When you read this anthology ask yourself when was the last time you painted, danced, dressed up, pretended to fly, pretended to be fairies, pretended to be a monster, made things out of boxes and made up stories?

Perhaps you too would like to go on a course at the Folk House.

Lucy English
Novelist and Lecturer in Creative Writing at Bath Spa University.

Introduction by Rosemary Dun

"There remains in circulation a myth that writing can't be taught. That despite the proliferation of writing courses, creative writing is something esoteric, unpindownable, something inspired by muses and shaped by genius. You've either got it or you haven't, so there's little point in trying to teach it." (The Creative Writing Coursebook, eds Julia Bell & Paul Magrs, pub Macmillan 2001). Yet, the success of many creative writing courses explodes this myth. No-one would deny that visual arts and music can be taught. The same applies to creative writing.

The basis of my writing courses is to pass on all the tips I've learnt over the years and to impart all I wish I'd known when I first started out as a writer. When I moved to Bristol I enrolled in a creative writing class at The Folk House and carried on from there. Adult education centres offer the unique opportunity for students to come along to learn for life and to have fun whilst doing so. Whether my students merely want to write for themselves as a hobby or are taking their first steps to a career as a writer makes no difference. Learning for learning's sake remains a valid if not important reason for embarking on adult education classes. And The Folk House is unique as it's an independent adult education co-operative not subject to government diktats. This means that Kate Gardiner and myself, in common with the other tutors, all construct our own courses.

So, why the anthology? I well remember when I first came out as a writer. "I'm a writer," I'd say – boldly – at some party, and inevitably would come the next question. "So, have you been published?" And, as I wasn't published at the time, I'd mutter: "Not yet." And the questioner would slink off to find someone more interesting. Now, with eighteen years of writing under my belt, I know how hard it is to get short stories into print, and how exciting and affirming it is to be able to answer: "Yes, I am published." But it still rankles. If you're in a band, people don't say: "Ah, but do you have a recording contract?" Or if a visual artist: "And where do you exhibit?" It's hard enough to take oneself seriously as a writer, and so this anthology was born because both Kate Gardiner and myself feel that many fine writers come through our courses who deserve the encouragement and buzz which being a published author can give.

Cut back to the beginning of my journey. When I began there were few creative writing courses, and even fewer tutors who knew what they were doing. I'd attend groups, workshops, writers conferences, in my search for the holy grail: my quest to discover the secrets which "proper" writers' must know, i.e. how to structure a story, how to find my voice, and how to work out the writing equivalent of the off-side rule – viewpoint. Someone somewhere must be able to pass on the magic formula. The truth is that in order to be a writer you have to write. There are no shortcuts, but there certainly are tools and tips which can be passed on, and which make the whole process less confusing.

We all have busy lives. Even published and successful writers, more often than not, have other jobs. This is an important lesson for emerging writers to know. And that the phenomenal success of JK Rowling is – well, a phenomenon – a one-off, and that large advances are the equivalent of winning the lottery. People can always find excuses for not writing. The most common of which is time. I've lost count of the number of occasions on which someone said, on being told that I'm writing a novel: "Oh, I could write a novel too. If only I had the time." Thereby offering up an excuse, whilst at the same time implying that, because I do write, I'm a wastrel with plenty of time on my hands: or that their life is far more interesting and packed full than mine.

A main objective, then, of my courses is to help new and returning writers to develop that "itch". To develop a regular writing routine so that if you're not writing there's a damned itch dying to be scratched.Once you have that itch then you're part way there.

"Where do your stories come from?" is a common question asked of writers. I try and instill confidence in my students that their stories will come. That they are there. This is what makes human beings so special. We make sense of our world by telling stories: whether chatting on the phone to a good friend about our day, passing on some gossip, or retelling a family tale. Stories are woven into the fabric of our everyday. The artist, whether a writer, a photographer, a musician, a dancer, tells stories through their own particular medium. Through structured exercises and the practice of freewriting my students are encouraged to work their subconscious from which all creativity flows.

The wondrous thing about being a writer is that there are always new discoveries to be made on your journey. I enjoy the journey of fledgling writers who join my courses, and am inspired and always learning from them too. The bringing together of this collection has been a new challenge full of hard slogs, tests, and in the end – triumph. We are very proud of all the students showcasing their work here. The vast majority are beginning writers and many are names to watch out for. Writers from previous classes have gone on to be published or to successfully complete MA courses in creative writing. There is a broad range of styles in this collection. Again, something we are proud of. Stories of mystery such as Stephanie Dobbie's "Mad Cow", through to a surreal tale "Clara" by Nathalia Gjersoe, a gay cowboy story by Tamar Zak, and the beautifully lyrical story "Rain" by Jenny May Forsyth. As well as fiction, both Kate Gardiner and I teach poetry, and I teach performance poetry and novel writing. So in this anthology we have included a delightful mix of poetry, including haiku from Roy Hilliar, a pastiche of "Talking Heads" by Ross Rossiter, and childhood memories from Caroline Ward.

Which brings us to that other old question: Can anybody write? Certainly anyone can be taught the creative processes involved in writing. These include the craft – or ways of doing – and the art – ways of seeing/ perceiving. Does this mean that creative writing classes will produce a plethora or writers? Hardly. And why not? Because many people enrol on classes like ours purely for their own personal pleasure. (And why not?) Many will leave and find those old reasons and excuses damping down their desire to write: family and work commitments, and the biggest of them all – time. So, no, it's unlikely that we shall be deluged by writers. What is more likely is that those who would have written in any case will continue, but with tools, techniques and tips to inspire and motivate. Being a writer takes a good deal of dedication and time. To be a writer one has to be in it for the long game. There are only a miniscule number of writers who are overnight successes – and even these are mainly labelled as such for the purpose of marketing hype. Chances are they have two, three, twenty previously written novels hidden in their bottom drawer. What creative writing classes can do is to give writers the wherewithal: the tools, the motivation and the lessons learnt by those who have gone before. It is then up to the individual to do with them what they will. The main thing which divides those who do and those who don't is not only the intention, but more importantly the willingness to develop "a writer's itch" and to put in the time. As Natalie Goldberg said in her book *Writing Down The Bones:"Writers write: everybody else makes excuses."*

We hope that you enjoy this showcase of The Folk House creative writing students. Maybe one day we'll see you at one of our classes.

Rosemary Dun
Creative Writing Tutor at the Folk House

Introduction by Kate Gardiner

Firstly I'd like to thank Rosemary for coming up with the inspiration for the Folk House Anthology. Not only does it give students a real opportunity to get their work published but it's a great showpiece for the unique creative enterprise that is the Bristol Folk House. I'd also like to thank all the students who submitted work to be considered for inclusion, it was wonderful to receive such a positive response. As a teacher of creative writing at the Folk House since I finished my Creative Writing MA in 2000, I've been terrifically lucky to be able to design and run the courses that I feel will help and inspire those who want to write and share their stories, in whatever poetic or narrative form they choose. Over the years I've met a huge number of students and had the opportunity to share some of my ideas and obsessions with them. Being a writer can be a lonely business and it's been a great privilege for me to work with so many talented and creative students. Plus I've had the chance to talk to a captive audience about two of my great passions; the short story and poetry.

I don't think there are many things to compete with the terror of joining a creative writing class and having to share your writing with a group of strangers. For many students this is the first time they will have written anything, let alone read it aloud and been given feedback on it. At the start of term I tell my students I'd like them to have finished three or four complete pieces by the end of it. I liken this to a pottery class, you'd expect by the end of term to have a pot, an ashtray, maybe even a milk jug. You'd have worked with the raw clay, shaped it, baked it, glazed it, polished it and have something completely unique by the end of it. It's a bit like that with a creative writing class, supplying the prompts to get the imagination going and helping the students to shape and mould those ideas to form the most beautiful 'pots' they can. As a teacher it's really important to me that my students feel more confident, informed about the creative process and more able to give and receive feedback by the end of term. There's also something uniquely wonderful about watching a group of students come together and form a small writing community over a number of weeks. Most writers need some support and help with the development of their craft and the Folk House courses offer not only that but a chance for students to meet other writers and share ideas and resources too.

For any writer the development of their own critical and editorial judgment is key. In my course Reading and Writing the Short Story we look at the work of some of the most well known exponents of the form and some lesser-known ones too. That's because I want my students to become more aware of the infinite ways in which a story can be told and be exposed to new ideas and approaches. If you can answer the questions: what's this story about, what are its strengths and weaknesses, what can I learn from this, then you can develop and extend those ideas and apply them to your own work. All writers are searching for their voice, and a chance to say, this is my story and I've written it in the way I want and in the most unique and honest way I can.

But equally important for writers is the need to be kind to the part of us that writes, to liberate ourselves from the critical monkey that sits on our shoulder and mocks, you can't do this, who wants to hear your story, your writing's so rubbish. Sound familiar? Writers need to find ways to break away from that and to encourage and nurture their creative spirit. I try and foster my students' creative impulses and encourage them to play with new ideas. If writing becomes all about editing, with none of the joy of creating, then the writing will have no spirit, no pulse.

Choosing which pieces to include in the anthology was incredibly difficult. There were so many diverse and interesting voices to choose from, so many imaginative ideas and threads. I was looking for originality and vibrancy, the pieces that left me thinking after I'd read them. It's that elusive quality that continues to haunt the reader long after the first read which makes a story or poem great.

My advice to students whose work wasn't included would be not to overlook the importance of editing. There were lots of pieces with fantastic potential, interesting characters, beguiling plots, good ideas but which fell short through a lack of rigorous shaping and editing. But mostly I would encourage everyone to keep going, keep writing and working at it. It can be gruelling and there are hundreds of distractions out there but the reward is knowing you've pushed yourself to be the best writer you can be.

I hope you enjoy reading the first Folk House Anthology and feel inspired to come along and join a course here, in creative writing, or in one of the other creative fields: art, music, pottery, whatever sets your creative flame alight and inspires you to pick up a pen and say, to hell with the critical monkey, I'm going to have a go.

Kate Gardiner
Creative Writing Tutor at the Folk House

Tamar Zak

Drift

So I was sittin there watchin that *Brokeback* movie. Staring at that old guy's body, dead in the ravine, with his dick ripped right out from between his legs. And my stomach just sank. Eighty years a life and what the hell's he got for it? Nuthin. They didn't even bury him. Just left him there. A goddamn feast for the flies and coyotes. The weird thing was when I was watchin it, all I kept thinkin 'bout was how that old queer guy had somebody. Some other cowboy guy called Ray. Somebody that fuckin loved him. I mean, ain't that typical. Those two old birds probably had nuthin in the world but each other, and some other bastard comes along and ruins it for 'em. Bastards. I swear, people don't want ya to have goddamn nuthin in this life. The world's fulla goddamn bastards, that's what it is.

I can relate to the kid, though. Ennis. Not the liking guys part. I'm not into guys or nuthin. I mean about how he was when he was a boy. About his dad and shit. My dad was just like that. Woulda done somethin just like that. Dragged me out to the middle of nowhere to see some dead fag's body, hand clenched around my neck and shit. I could almost feel that guy's fuckin hand around my neck when I saw it. I mean it.

That's why I came out here, y'know. Had to get away. The old man was on my case all the time. Who needs it? He'd kick my head in if he coulda seen me tonight, though. Sittin in some fuckin queer movie in the middle of the goddamn city. He'd split his fuckin gut about it. That's why I went, if you wanna know. Just so I could sit there picturin him splittin his gut about me being at a goddamn queer flick. Ha. But I wasn't expectin the dead guy. Uh uh. I thought it'd be like lotsa fairies in pink and shit fallin off their horses. Thought it'd be kinda funny, y'know? Gay cowboys. Yeah right. It ain't, though. Funny, I mean. Not really.

But anyway, it ain't like I never seen gay shit before. There was a kid at my Junior High who had it. Skinny kid. They used to put him in the dumpsters out back after school. Throw him in there with all the garbage and stuff from lunch. I came by once when he was stuck in there bangin on the lid. Boy did he stink when I got him out. Decent kid, though. He used to help me out with my homework sometimes after that. On the low, like. Not so anybody knew. That kinda shit can kill ya, hangin out with a faggot. Don't know what ever happened to that kid. Just stopped showing up one day. First I reckoned maybe that Johnny kid got him, the one that used to put him in the trash. God knows he talked about it enough. But nobody ever said nuthin about it, not even the teachers. I figure he musta moved. Lucky bastard. Maybe I shoulda been a queer just so I coulda got outta that place sooner. Maybe it woulda helped.

Anyway man, you woulda liked the way I got out here. Didn't have nuthin. Ten bucks is all. My old man said to me before I left, 'You ain't never gonna make it nowhere on ten bucks.' I did, though. Hitched all the way. You'd probably call that charity. You'd probably say see, now that's an example of the good shit that can happen in this world. It ain't, though. It's just luck. That's how it is with me. Somethin good happens, like me getting out here, and then somethin real bad'll happen right on the back of it. New York though, I swear. I always wanted to go to New York. I caught a ride with this old trucker on the way out here. When I told him where I was headed, he just smiled and started whistlin that old Sinatra song. Kept rollin on through the darkness. Man, I ain't never seen nuthin like it – just miles and miles a highway and stars. Felt like I coulda gone on that way forever. Didn't even go to sleep. Just stayed up watchin the sky till daybreak, when all that color and light come sweepin in on us. I couldn't help smilin to myself, y'know. And then I started thinkin 'bout how the old man said I weren't never gonna make it. How I was gonna rot and die back there just like him. Well, sit and spin, baby. That's all I gotta say 'bout that. Sit and spin.

I figure, if I wanted to stick around for a while, I could go and fix up a little work for myself tomorrow. Not that I'd need to. See I reckon you can get most things in life free, if ya gotta. Like I screwed this girl last night, she works at the movie place. That's

1

how I got in. Didn't pay for it or nuthin. She was all right, that girl. Name's Destiny. How 'bout that for a name, huh? Fuckin Destiny. Bet her ma was higher than hell when she came up with that one. But yeah, she was all right, man. She was one a those artsy type girls. You know the ones I mean. Got all these posters up all over her apartment, of like old movie stars and stuff. Jimmy Dean. Marilyn. That kinda thing. Classic. I didn't even try it on with her or nuthin. She came over to me. I was hangin round this place downtown, shootin the shit with the bartender, trying to get a drink outta it, when this Destiny chick rocks up and offers to buy me one. Cute girl, really. Said she liked my hat. Said I reminded her a someone she used to know. Whatever, don't matter to me. Saved me sleepin on the street's all I know.

Then this morning, she tells me she's got the afternoon off. Offers to take me round the city. Showed me the Statue of Liberty, Empire State Building. We even went down to where the towers used to be. Hung out down there for a while. That's some crazy shit, man. All that empty air. I sure remember the day they went down. Never seen the old guy so quiet in my whole damn life. Just sat there all day drinkin beer and watchin the news. Man, they musta played those clips a the planes crashin in 'bout a million times. The old man never said nuthin, though. Almost felt like we didn't hate each other no more. Fuckin crazy shit man. Crazy. Don't know where the fuck *you* were when all that shit was goin on, man. Said that to Destiny today. And you know what she said? Said she reckons you don't even exist. Thinks somebody made you up. How the hell's somebody gonna make up Jesus? I said. What about all those people that knew him? Saw him do all those miracles, walk on water and shit. Uh uh. How the hell's somebody gonna make somethin like that up? Ain't no way.

She went kinda funny on me after that, so I bought her a slice a pizza for lunch. That was my last $2.50 outta my ten bucks. I always wanted to eat pizza with a pretty girl in New York though, so I figured that was all right. She was a pretty cool girl too. You know, besides all that artsy shit. Even sings in a band or somethin.

2

I think that's all right, y'know. When I was back home I always wanted to be in a band. I can play like Hendrix man, serious. Used to sit around for hours practicin, 'till the bastard come home drunk one night and busted up my guitar. I betcha if I wanted to I could start somethin up now that I'm here. Bet I could be famous one day. That'd show the old guy. Yeah, he wouldn't be able to talk no shit then, no way.

Anyway, that's how I got out here. Not that you care or nuthin. Not that it matters. I know you got bigger shit on your plate than me. I just figured I oughtta check in before I did it. So's you'd understand and everythin. So you wouldn't take it personal. It ain't personal, I just ain't got the patience for it. I don't wanna end up like that old guy in the movie. Find somethin to make me happy, just so as some bastard can come take it away from me. Ain't worth it. Rather just let it all stay safe up in my head. Least I got to see New York, though. Man, I always wanted to see New York. I called the old man, y'know. Right before I came out here tonight. I called him up and said, 'I fuckin made it ya stupid bastard, so how 'bout that?' I almost told him that I turned fuckin queer too, just to really piss'm off. But I didn't. I just hung up. He won't ever know nuthin, 'cept that I made it. Maybe the guy that pulls my body outta this damn river'll call him up and let'm know his kid's dead. I got the number in my wallet. They'd find it if they looked.

Yeah, so anyway, man. Thanks for nuthin. The world's fulla bastards that's all I gotta say – city or no city. Still, it's kinda crazy. I mean, here I am and I just can't stop thinkin 'bout this river. I mean, just look at it. Just look at it, man. Like the way the lights are. Y'know, just kinda dancin around on the water like that. The way they're just kinda flickerin away like that. Almost like they're kinda wonderin 'bout somethin. I mean, what d'ya reckon their wonderin about, man? You reckon they're wonderin 'bout why they stay in the same place all the time? You know, like night after night and stuff. Always flickerin off the same spot. Cuz that water man, it's movin. I mean, it ain't gonna stop. It's just gonna keep on going that way, y'know. Keep on runnin.

Tighe O'Connor

A Step In The Right Direction

'I am holding still dammit, look you're pulling the wrong way, just leave it alone, it'll have to do.' I recognise the last minute nerves in my colleague's attempts to help, but hell I am the one who got lumbered with this contraption.

It all sounded so easy in the pub with a couple of malt whiskies behind me and that good-looking barmaid listening to all the banter. She was far too young for me. They all are these days. The others didn't think the old git could do it. So naturally, when the choice for who was going to be first came, I had to do it – I'll show 'em, those young whippersnappers. I thought. At the time.

This Big Ben frame is bloody heavy. 'Light as a breeze,' someone says. Don't know what breeze they are talking about. The people just up ahead of us are finally moving. Here we go then. No way out now.

I start walking with the crowd. We are all one slowly moving mess of colours, like lava flow – and just about the right speed. After a while the first few try to run but are defeated by the ebb and flow of the many, quite content to have these last seconds of contemplation. Soon enough we will turn to joggers, then finally runners. My vision in this thing is pretty limited. Instead of a clock face, my already ruddy face sticks out and it's fairly impossible to turn.

What I want to know is whose bright idea was it to dress up as Big Ben and run 26 miles? I know it's the London Marathon and for charity but there's stupid and there's….My thoughts trail off as I finally begin to run. The first steps come awkwardly as the light wood and canvas gently sways left, then right. Though it's only nine thirty am, the sweat is trickling down my face. Already.

I try to establish some sort of rhythm but my knees clatter against the damn frame which obviously wasn't built for a fifty seven year old cigar-smoking, whiskey-drinking, gout-ridden fat git like me. But, here I am. Making progress – albeit slowly – which pleases

4

me as I keep getting in the way of a lot of eager masochists…I'll probably step over them later on when they've hit their wall. My confidence is rising, then decreases rapidly when I pass a sign with big bold letters **'STARTING LINE'.** No. I must have run at least a mile. Can't they take that off the end?

'Hello Douglas. You're doing excellent. Really good stuff, old chap. Keep it up.' Its at this point that I make what'll probably be the first of many attempts to topple Big Ben in the direction of my very unwise running colleague. I have the feeling that it's going to be a long day.

The plan is for me – Staff Sergeant Douglas T. Aikerman, previously to be found in times past restoring Law & Order by gentle or more rudimentary persuasion in the killing fields of the world, and now more likely to be the cause of unlawful disorder in any number of local hostelries, (well the ones I'm still not barred from) – to run the first third of this godawful race.

What gets me, right, is that ordinary civilians think that by running and completing, they have achieved something of note! And the organisers even give them medals for it! What complicity. I hate that "everyone's a winner," rubbish. What sort of world is this? And where's my medal, then, for doing the honourable thing and knocking a few heads together for Queen & Country, eh?

'Ok Dougie Boy? Hanging on in there?' wheezes Lee, displaying the type of heavy breathing most phone perverts would be proud of. This thought heartens me no end. Mind you, Lee's idea of training is to walk to the chippy instead of taking the car. A true athlete for modern times.

Runners have been shouting their encouragement as they pass, and it's strangely affecting to hear the common herd standing along the way shouting me on. Although I'm pretty sure that little kid shouted: 'Come on fat Ben.'

There's men standing outside public houses, pints in hand. They remind me of me - their stomachs bursting through T-shirts, as they grin and burst into song every now and again. I'm touched. But also deeply envious of their proximity to alcohol. Luckily I can

5

feel the little stowaway hipflask of finest Glenfiddich wedged in the wooden frame just above me. For emergencies, naturally. I suppose you might think I'm a bit of an old soak? You could be right, but isn't everyone a binge drinker these days? To me everyone needs a pick-me-up now and again. I just need more pick-me-ups than most.

Five miles in, and I'm not feeling too bad, all things considered. The conversation of my fellow runners, though, has now slowed to the odd quickly spoken comment.

'Drinks up ahead, Douglas,' splutters Lee.

Momentarily, the image of a rather large gin and tonic wafts before me. The image is strong. I can smell the slice of lemon that floats tantalising amongst the ice cubes. Instead I'm handed a small bag of something called Isotonic.

'Err, what the hell's this?' I gurgle, as I try to spit it out and end up making a mess down the front of Big Ben.

'It's a sports drink,' says Trevor. 'To help your muscles.'

'Tell you what. You be a good sport and get me some plain old-fashioned water.'

The heat of the day is rising. As I'm carrying probably the heaviest costume, I'm obviously the first to notice it. I'm not sure where we are exactly at this point. I remember passing by the beautiful Cutty Sark at Woolwich. Maybe we're around Bermondsey – it definitely smells like it.

Must Keep Focused. Tower Bridge is my target. My pace quickens, and although I don't quite leave Trevor, Lee and Roger in my tracks, I do take comfort in the puffing and panting that spells their discomfort. Running is a wonderful leveller, I'd just forgotten how much. It also allows you to separate the mind and body and think about allsorts of ideas in your quest to not think of aching shins, feet, back, and in particular, knees. Maybe Buddhists should take up running instead of long hours of meditation. Surely it can't be good on the muscles, can it? All that sitting around chanting?

'I say, Roger, do you think he's alright?' I hear Trevor ask.

'Of course I'm alright you damn infidels,' I say. 'I haven't

6

felt this good since I charged the enemy in sixty-eight. We were outnumbered that's for sure, and not even a mention in dispatches. There's gratitude.'

'Not you, Dougie,' interrupts Roger. 'It's Lee. He's barely walking.'

'I'll be alright,' comes the pitiful response. 'It's just blisters. And a touch of cramp.'

'Course you'll be alright,' I say. 'I had to walk seventeen miles once with a bit of a flesh-wound. And carrying Fraser. He'd taken a real tonking and wasn't exactly the lightest load known to mankind.'

And again, barely a mention in dispatches – I swear that Major Faffbrothy-Jenkins never liked me.

'Anyway, Lee,' I manage to get out, as running and talking don't really mix. 'Take it easy for the next mile and we'll swap the costume after Tower Bridge. You're next to take over.' I'll be glad to get this costume off, I can tell you.

'I don't think Lee's in any shape to take over at the moment, Dougie,' says Roger. 'Do you mind carrying on for a while, and then Trevor can take it further down the road?'

'Ok. Agreed,' I say, a bit out of puff myself now. I don't quite like the ring of further down the road.

Tower Bridge finally looms into sight and although we're walking to help Lee back into the race, I'm not too miffed. The sight of all those runners is a joy to behold and I'm caught up in the excitement and glad to be part of it. Time for a swig of finest Glenfidich me thinks. After a while we resume running. I'm a bit disappointed that there's no star interviewer in sight. I haven't seen Jimmy Saville either – but one must, I suppose, be grateful for small mercies.

It's clear that Lee has become dead wood and must be cut free in order to ensure the survival of the rest. Like Captain Oates with Scott in the Antarctic. Even Lee senses this. 'I'm going over to the side of the road,' he tells us. 'I may be some time.'

I feel like we're running standing still. Canary Wharf seems to be everywhere. We obviously are running because that twit Trevor goes and trips over a water bottle then sprawls in front of me – almost toppling me. Instead he takes out Batman & Robin to my left far better than any of their comic adversaries ever could. Batman shouts something very un-Bruce-Wayne at him.

I stop to survey the damage as runners scatter left and right of us. Comradeship's a bit thin on the ground, I think, as I watch them hurtle past, but the marshals are quick to rush to the scene.

'Dougie, bad news,' says Roger. 'Trevor's twisted his knee. So he's out of it. Just you and me now. Can you carry on with that Big Ben thing?' I can hear him loud and clear by my side. 'You are coping tremendously, mate. You know I'd take over in a shot if it weren't for my bad back.'

Bad back indeed, I think. 'Look Roger, everything's fine. There's no can't on my watch. I can do it all right.'

Suddenly I'm aware of how much I'm enjoying this. The crowds cheering us on; the colours; the sense of doing something worthwhile; the getting drawn into the good nature of the spectators; the mere barmy spectacle of it all; and the discovery that I might actually be connected to the human race slightly more than I had previously imagined. So instead of hitting that wall of pain they talk about, I'm actually smiling.

Running around Canary Wharf, though, is taking its toll on both Roger. me and the runners about us. There's not much conversation now. Mile-marking mostly. Even the crowd has thinned out. I see a sign which says **Mile Twenty-two**. In the quiet of pounding feet, my thoughts drift. It's funny the things that appear from nowhere, I'm suddenly right back to a stiflingly hot May 16th 1965. Nervous as hell, legs like jelly. Maybe that's why I remember it; a fresh-faced 18 year old on his first day in the army, standing straight as possible, trying not to breathe whilst the Sergeant shouts his welcoming speech. At one point he comes right up to my face, almost touching mine, then says quietly - as if talking to me alone – 'Son, when I have finished training you, you will be able to run through brick walls.'

This pleases my scrawny eighteen year old self no end.

Back to the run, and Roger and I pass each other some small words of encouragement. He's surprised me a lot today. I had him down as the first to drop out. I tell him so, as well. Suppose you shouldn't judge a book by its battered cover. He tells me you can't judge Big Ben by its short stubby legs! Cheeky git.

My legs are concerning me, though. Even more so since I drained that hipflask at mile 19. Not too far to go now. We pass tube stations, people, and I can smell the end in sight. Up ahead I hear a man calling out some of the runners' names, geeing them up for the final 'Beecher's Brook'. I reckon I can make it when my legs start going in opposite directions and I lurch slightly to the right – gently clipping an American runner. I ascertain he's American by his colourful language.

Next I lurch to the left and accidentally whack Roger.

'Sorry, old boy,' I say. Legs misbehaving, I grind to a halt. Stationary seems an improvement. I dare to take one step forward and regret my haste immediately as neither leg seems to be on speaking terms with the other.

We're so close, I groan. Mile 25 is just ahead. I'm not going to be beaten by my own body. What does it know anyway? I look around for inspiration and let my gaze fall on the crowd next to us. They are calling encouragement. They don't want to see us fail…. And they won't, I decide.

Two stewards stand nearby, so I send Roger over with instructions. Glad to be pressed into service they return pushing just what I need to finish.

'Plonk yerself in that,' says Roger, all enthusiastic now.

I don't think the sight of a wheelchair has ever been more welcome to me.

I lower myself in. Still keeping the Big Ben contraption on, it's like a second skin now – I point forward and jokingly bellow: 'Tally ho, old boy!' The crowd cheer and take up the chant – 'Tally ho.' Poor old Roger, I think. Not only does he have to drag his body – which must be hurting everywhere – but he's got to push me too.

9

Still. That's teamwork, eh?

'AND HERE COMES RUNNER 30274, DOUGLAS AIKERMAN, WHO'S DRESSED AS BIG BEN. LADIES AND GENTLEMEN, GIVE THESE TWO A BIG CHEER AS THEY PASS. THEY'VE DONE REALLY REALLY WELL.'

A big holler goes up and my spirits rise.

And now running alongside is that celebrity interviewer: 'Hi guys,' she says. 'Do you mind if I run along with you and do a little interview for the BBC?'

'No, no not at all,' stammers Roger.

Because Kirsty Gallacher in the flesh is even more beautiful than I imagined. Much better than on the telly. Bold, I ask: 'Kirsty. Would you mind finishing this race with us?'

'Sure,' replies the goddess, with a little laugh.

'Hi everyone,' says Kirsty to the camera whilst helping Roger push me in my chair. 'I'm here in the final mile with Roger and Douglas.' She points the microphone in my direction. 'Douglas, let me ask you. Why Big Ben?'

Damn. What she ask that for?

'Well Kirsty I…well we…' I search for a reason. 'Um, we just wanted to stand out a bit for the folks back home.' I finally reply. Relieved.

'And where's home for you boys?' she asks.

'Och, only the greatest town in Somerset, Kirsty. Frome. All the lads will be packed into the Drowned Rat on Milk Street watching this,' I say – hoping that they are.

'So, are you boys raising any money for charity today?' continues the ever–professional Kirsty.

'We are…' breaks in Roger. And for once, I am grateful to the lad. In eloquent tones, Roger explains how much we have raised for the hospice and why we are here raising money in the first place. To honour our good friend Harry – Roger's dad and former owner of the Drowned Rat till his recent death. Maybe I'd shut this out – the bit about Harry's death – but the emotion in Roger's voice brings it all back to me.

The crowd cheers us on and the beautiful end is in sight. We cross the line to even bigger cheers. I've read somewhere that there are seventy-six pubs on this marathon. Maybe next time I'll drink my way round them all. A charity pub crawl – that sounds a much more civilised thing to do. Harry would like that.

I must admit, though, that when I got that medal placed around my neck I was pretty emotional. Very unlike me. At least this time I'll get a mention in dispatches.

Stephanie Dobbie

Mad Cow

Right on cue the call came in. It always happened when he was on his way home at the end of a long shift. He had learnt to live with it. It was part of the job after all. He heard a voice over the crackling radio.

'McAvoy, do you read me? Come in, McAvoy.'

He hesitated to pick up the call, he had plans for tonight, but now they'd have to wait.

'This is McAvoy,' he said.

'They've found a woman's body in Blaysdon Woods, how soon can you get there?'

'Ten minutes.'

'Okay, the Inspector will meet you there. Over and out.'

McAvoy slipped his car into gear and did a sharp tyre-screeching u-turn. He accelerated down the narrow country road which led to the woods. When he arrived it was already dark. The Forensics team had started work.

How the hell did they get here so quick? he thought.

Powerful flashlight beams darted across the sky. He wondered what on earth they were doing. They're meant to be looking for a murderer not bloody UFOs. Then he heard a familiar voice behind him.

'McAvoy.'

He turned around to see Inspector Burns stood there.

'Terrible business,' Burns said. 'Awful state she was in.'

'Any details yet sir?'

'Not really, so far we haven't been able to identify her. Her fingers were cut off, so no prints. Teeth been removed too. And the eyes.'

McAvoy turned to watch Forensics at work. They always fascinated, but sometimes angered him too. He knew that they were good at their job, but they didn't think like a detective. They were scientists who dealt with logic, two plus two equals four stuff, whereas he dealt with the unpredictable side of human nature.

The woods seemed hostile to McAvoy. As if the sound of rustling leaves were a voice, daring him to enter into the blackness ahead. He waited until his eyes became accustomed to the dark, and then he began scanning the trees, looking for clues, but also remembering the last time he was here. The trees shielded a clearing which had been used to burn cow carcasses during the foot and mouth epidemic. He had been called here one day to assist. A local farmer had lost his entire herd to the disease, and then had to watch as they were piled into a heap and set alight. The farmer had threatened to throw himself onto the fire, but in the end was too busy crying his eyes out. Poor old sod, he'd thought at the time.

The air was cold, causing McAvoy to pull his black three-quarter length coat tight around him. He never buttoned it. He needed access to his inside pockets at all times. He carried a battered notebook, a black biro, and a set of handcuffs in his top pocket. His lower pocket contained an unopened pack of cigarettes, which he did not smoke. He kept them in case he needed to put a suspect at ease. Sometimes only a cigarette would do. He also carried his police radio, and a giant set of keys, which had taken him twelve years on the force to collect. He couldn't remember where most of them had come from, but kept them as souvenirs.

He took a handkerchief from one of the other officers then followed the Inspector into the woods. He didn't mind looking at decomposing bodies, but he couldn't stand the smell.

The woodland floor was damp. He could feel the moisture seeping through a hole in his comfortable leather shoes, which he'd meant to get fixed last week. Up ahead, flashlights traced the treetops.

'Sir, why are they looking up there?'

'Some of her clothing was found in the trees,' Burns said. 'God knows how they got up there. Do you know, the Chief suggested some sort of ape might have attacked her. Maybe an illegal pet that had gotten loose, he said. Even had me get one of the lads to check

13

zoos for escapees.'

'Apes don't cut off peoples fingers, boss.'

'No. Of course not. And, anyway McAvoy, I've seen her. Only a human could've done that.'

He gave the Inspector a glance. Inspector Burns was a cynic with more than an occasional contempt for the whole of the human race.

They reached the crime scene which was taped off. The body was hidden from view by a tent, giving the victim a final piece of dignity. A dozen or so people went about their jobs like it was business as usual. Which it was, for them, I suppose, thought McAvoy. He didn't blame them; he knew the score. You couldn't afford to become emotionally involved if you wanted to stay sane. His head was beginning to ache due to the bright artificial lights surrounding the crime scene. He pulled back the tent flap and walked inside.

It stank. Just as he'd known it would. He placed the handkerchief over his mouth and coughed. He knelt down beside the victim and made himself look at her rotting face. He could see into the skull. There were teeth marks where a small animal had eaten part of the tissue. Her facial structure had caved in due to the removal of teeth, and the remaining skin on her hands was turning green.

He looked down her body, and saw that she was still wearing some clothing.

'I thought her clothes were found up a tree?' he said.

'Some were,' said his boss. 'Forensics have taken a sample of this cloth. We may get something from it.'

McAvoy closely examined it. 'Pink and white gingham,' he muttered. 'Now where have I seen this before?'

He walked outside, filling his lungs with fresh air as he looked up at the star-filled sky, then smiled. The Inspector emerged from the tent to join him.

'The last time I saw a sky like this, sir, was up at that farm last week,' he said. 'It's a shame what happened to that farmer. First his cows go mad, and then his wife takes off. It's very quiet up there at his farm. Not much human contact I should think.' He looked at his boss. 'You'd like that sir, eh?'

'Ha bloody ha. Now what are you holding onto that cloth for?'

A cold wind blew McAvoy's collar up against his neck, then continued to disarrange his thick dark hair. His weathered face resisted the onslaught, as he narrowed his eyes against the elements. It was then that he knew for sure.

'I'm pretty certain I know where I've seen this cloth before, sir.'

'Where?'

'I think its best if I show you, sir.'

'Do you mind telling me just where it is that we're going?' asked Inspector Burns, as he nevertheless followed his Sergeant out of the woods.

'I'll explain in the car, sir.'

Twenty minutes later they pulled up outside a remote farmhouse.

'If you don't mind sir, I think I should do the talking. He knows me.'

Inspector Burns stared at McAvoy, then nodded. 'Okay, lad. You lead the way.'

McAvoy got out of the car and felt how fresh the air was. He pulled his coat tighter to keep out the cold, then looked into the distance at the outline of High Water Hills undulating across the sky. I'm lucky I can still look at that view, he thought. That woman in the woods is not so lucky.

Determined, he turned and headed for the farmhouse, closely followed by his Inspector, clearly signalling that he had his confidence.

The ground was covered by sharp-edged stones, which cut into McAvoy's foot through the hole in his shoe. It felt like razor blades were pressing into his sole, causing him to wince at each step. As the two men climbed the path to the front door, they heard the sound of a whistling kettle from inside the farmhouse.

'Sounds like we're right on cue,' said Burns, with a wry smile on his face.

McAvoy didn't respond to his boss's attempt at humour, instead he pushed the door slightly. It was open.

He was about to knock, when a strong gust of wind flung the door inwards, causing it to smash against a heavy brass doorstop. McAvoy could see the farmer standing in front of a large wood-burning stove.

'I've been expecting you,' he said. 'Come on in. Kettle's just boiled.'

The two policemen entered and watched as the farmer poured boiling water into the teapot next to the stove. Three mugs were already placed on the kitchen table.

'We need to have a word,' said McAvoy. His boss walked over to the window, letting him do the talking.

The farmer continued his tea-making. He placed the teapot, milk jug and sugar basin on a tray then carried it over to the table. He sat, then motioned to the men to join him. 'Why don't you come and sit down?' he said. 'Tea's all ready.'

Outside the wind was whipping up a frenzy, whistling down the chimney as if doing battle with the open fire in the hearth. McAvoy noticed the fire was holding its own. Instead of accepting the farmer's invitation he walked over to warm himself by the hot coals. In the middle of the mantelpiece sat a photograph. He picked it up. There, sat on a garden bench, and surrounded by red rose bushes, was the farmer and his wife. The farmer had his arm placed gently around his wife's shoulders, and their heads were leaning against each other in a clear display of affection. Both wore broad smiles, as sunny as the weather, on the day the photograph was taken. She wore a dress of pink and white gingham.

McAvoy turned the picture for his boss to see, then looked over at the farmer, who was slouched over the table, head in hands. The farmhouse door swung open again. This time the wind had its way and quenched the fire. The temperature in the kitchen fell as quickly as a mortally wounded soldier.

McAvoy placed the photograph back on the mantelpiece. 'So, what happened?' he asked.

The farmer's eyes, as he looked up, were bloodshot and glistened with tears. 'I had to do it, see?' he said. 'She were mad. A right mad cow, make no mistake.'

Roy Hilliar

Stillness

snow covered fields and dry stone walls,
a hilltop crowned by whispering trees,
a country lane and scurrying leaf,
a baby asleep at last,
a dried-up stream,
the sea between tides,
nations remembering the Asian tsunami.

On the Move

A tied dog and bike
lie on the moving backyard,
of narrow boat's roof.

Counter Weight

Alongside the bridge
two alpine horns lie silent.
Too heavy to lift.

Girl

Bright purple hair worn
in Rastafarian style,
over a tired dress.

Sunset

The setting sun slips
behind a distant hedgerow,
now burnt to charcoal.

Cathy Wilson

None today, thank you

They try and sell you anything on the doorstep these days. Must think we're all gaga. Jason probably took one look at his worksheet and thought it was his lucky day: I mean, Mulberry Drive? If that isn't the name of a road where people come to die I don't know what is.

Ordinarily I would have pretended deafness, waited for him to go away. Would I have answered the door, if I'd been feeling … stronger? Who knows.

* * *

He stood on the step, youngish-looking, quite smart – cheap suit and tie anyway – a document case under one arm. He was giving me a smile straight out of charm school. All this I could see through the spyhole. Of course, by the time I'd fiddled and got the locks undone and the safety chain off, the smile had faded. When I opened the door I don't know which of us was more surprised. He was even younger than I'd thought. Flawless skin. Lovely hands. He must have thought I looked grim, or something, because he immediately took a step backward. Then appeared to try and recover his composure. Sweet.

'Hello-d'you-have-a-moment?' Ah. It all came out as one piece: he'd rushed in too quick. Started to blush and looked at his cribsheet. 'Sorry, I should have introduced myself first. Er, I'm Jason and I represent *The Good Old Days* ...'

'You could have fooled me,' I said. 'You don't look much out of nappies.'

'No, it's the company I work for.' He waved a brochure at me. Mock Olde Worlde lettering, soft-focus sepia portraits. 'We specialise in memorabilia … creating personal artworks, so your special memories are preserved … for all time.'

For all time? That seemed an odd notion for someone his age. 'Are you to be one of my special memories then?' I said.

He shifted from one foot to the other. 'We use your own photographs, keepsakes, that sort of thing … er, oh I see. You were joking.' He gave a nervous laugh.

'Am I your first?' More nervous laughter from him. '*Customer*, dearie,' I said peering at him. He really did have the softest of skin. 'Am I your first customer?' By now he'd gone bright red to the roots of his beautiful blond hair and for a moment … well, for a moment it was as if I could feel time spin. He was so like … Then he smiled. A big sheepish grin this time. Almost girlish, but completely natural. I steadied myself against the door jamb as I'm no spring chicken myself. 'Look,' I said. 'Why don't you come in? I can't stand for much longer. We can have a nice sit down and a cup of tea.'

He said he wasn't supposed to go inside: company rules. So I said he'd not get much custom that way, and could suit himself, and 'Good Day'. I gave the door a little push not quite closing it, and went back inside – leaving him on the doorstep. Still, I couldn't resist peeking in the hall mirror on the way and having a little chuckle to myself. Ah. He looked crestfallen … no, more like *crushed* – in that way only the very young can look. I almost hated myself.

Of course, he followed me in, saying: 'Er, it'll be alright this once I suppose. And anyway, you left your door open. I thought I'd better let you know. You can't be too careful.'

'Oh, how silly of me.' I shook my head vaguely in what I hoped was a fair imitation of absent-mindedness. 'Thank you, dear. Do sit down. Can I get you some tea? I've just made a pot.'

He called through to the kitchen: 'You really must be more careful. I could have been anybody.' But you aren't, are you, I thought, practically licking my lips. You're perfectly wonderful and so, so young …

I brought out the tea. 'What were you saying?'

'About being careful …'

'Ah, yes. Of course, I could say the same about you, dear. Door to door sales … isn't that rather a risky occupation?'

21

'Not round here I wouldn't have thought.'

'Oh, we're all too feeble, I suppose. Past it, isn't that what you think?' Not so feeble I couldn't put you over my knee, if I've a mind to, I thought. Then, careful Zelda. Timing is everything. You don't want to scare him off.

The young man was trying to renew a business tone. 'So, madam,' he said. 'Do you feel you might be interested in looking at what we have to offer?'

What I felt was hungry. What I said was: 'What exactly is it you're selling?'

He placed his portfolio on my occasional table. 'Right. Well. Let's say you have a particular day you want to commemorate. A wedding perhaps?' I shook my head. He was way off course. 'Or a national celebration, like The Coronation.' He looked over at me. 'Do you have a special day you'd particularly like to remember?'

I wanted to tell him: 'Plenty, but the past is past.' Instead, I said: 'Well, if I already remember it, where exactly do you fit in? Have a chocolate biscuit, by the way.' He looked distracted. 'They're homemade...'

'Ah. No thanks. We're not supposed to eat on duty.'

'Oh, don't be ridiculous. Nobody's going to know, now are they? It'll be our secret.' I offered him the plate of biscuits. 'So, you were saying... special days. What about the Coronation of Queen Victoria?'

He picked up one of the biscuits. 'Don't you mean Queen Elizabeth?'

'I know the difference,' I said. Well, it didn't matter now. 'I'm not completely senile,' I couldn't resist saying.

'Sorry,' he said. 'It's just that … well … customers usually pick events … er, not so far back.'

'Then I suppose I'm not your usual customer. Have another biscuit.' He took one. 'Are you saying you don't go that far back?'

'In theory,' he said, waving his biscuit as he spoke, getting crumbs everywhere. I tried not to frown. 'I don't see a problem with Queen Victoria. Although, you don't look old enough. I must say.'

I smiled at him.

'I don't suppose you have a photograph of yourself from that time?'

'Well, seeing as photography was still in its infancy, then I'd have to say no. Do have another biscuit. They're delicious. Aren't they? Homemade.'

By now he was looking decidedly bleary-eyed. His words were beginning to slur: 'I'm wondering ... perhaps something ... less formal might suit you better. Private parties can be just as special as ... big ... events...'

'I see you're a good judge of character. How're the biscuits?'

'Delicious ... you not having any?'

'Oh no. I'm on a special diet, dear. I only make these for my visitors.'

* * *

He looked so lovely lying there on my little sofa, I hadn't the heart to move him. Still, I set about removing his tie, and undoing his collar so his long pale neck could gleam in the late afternoon sun. And then I just sat there and watched him. But as evening fell and my hunger grew unbearable I knew I couldn't put it off. There would be all the tidying up to do afterwards, which always feels rather shabby. Still, needs must, and ... well ... I always get over it. Only, this time would not be so easy. I could tell I wasn't thinking straight, because when it came to deciding what to do with his document case I wondered: should I return the customer response sheet in case there were any enquiries? Under where it says *Details of Order*, write 'None today, thank you'?

When I checked the order pad, I could see it was brand new and unmarked. Just like him. I really had been his first customer — he hadn't even started filling out the form. Lucky for me.

Cathy Wilson

Old Flame

You mean a lot to him –
that much is clear.
Why else would you remain
in this ruined,
once-ivoried
tower?

The steps
are worn
thin
and treacherous
as they wind upwards
skelter-helter.

You sit at the top
in black, hunched
over lost dreams;
spinning stories;
making sense of it all.

Dinah Foweraker

Ginger Beer

Alison and Simon had arranged to meet for lunch. They hadn't seen each other for over a month, not since the row. Simon couldn't even remember what it had been about now. Eventually, when he couldn't stand it any longer he'd phoned her and she suggested meeting up to talk things over. She'd sounded distant on the phone which was hardly surprising as before the row, he'd been trying to cool things down.

Now he was keen to patch things up. Even though he didn't like the way she introduced him as her 'partner' to strangers. For months now he'd been ignoring her hints about it being ridiculous keeping on two properties when she spent most of the time at his place. He'd managed to resist her moving in. Still, every time she came over for the night or weekend she brought a full suitcase and left with an empty one. The latest of her contraptions was in the bathroom. When he asked, he was informed it was a foot spa. He had no idea what a foot spa might be, and didn't like the sound of it.

To be honest, Simon wasn't into feet. He knew they were at the end of his legs, naturally. And that they stopped one falling over. Apart from that he was quite content to leave well alone. Except for occasionally cutting his toenails. Which reminded him how the row had started. Alison complaining about his toenail clippings in the shower. Or was it smelly socks?

Whatever. It had been something to do with feet.

Since the row the foot spa seemed to reproach him with its very presence, every time he went to the bathroom. Alison was too fastidious for her own good, he'd decided. But he had missed her.

So why not let her move in? Hm. It could make his times with Petra even more exciting. He couldn't really claim to have a mistress without first having a live-in girlfriend. Now, could he?

* * *

25

Alison was worrying about her forthcoming confrontation with Simon. She'd decided it was better to meet somewhere neutral. Lunch, at least, was finite; whereas dinner could drag on interminably.

The café was a few streets along from her workplace, tucked away from their usual wine-bar haunts where she and Simon might be overheard by a colleague or interrupted by one of Simon's rugger mates.

Before it was strictly necessary, she had her coat on and was striding out of the office. She arrived early at the café – picked unseen from *Yellow Pages*. Immediately she was disappointed. The exterior signalled the café's seediness. Inside it reeked of cheap frying oil. Covering the walls and ceiling was wood panelling, darkened by time and the greasy atmosphere. And the dim lighting did little to relieve the gloom. Curiously padded curtains and upholstery added to the impression of being inside an enormous coffin. In its heyday, she imagined the café had been an Edwardian teashop with waitresses in starched aprons attending well-groomed matrons. A hundred years on, it was surviving by selling breakfasts, lunches, buns and beverages to a motley assortment of old-age pensioners, the unemployed and people otherwise down on their luck, plus the odd tourist who'd strayed off the recommended heritage trail.

Alison waited. Simon was late. As usual. She decided to go ahead and order her meal anyway. It would save time. And, if necessary allow her to make a swift exit. Cod and chips, egg and chips, pie and chips, jacket potatoes, or dish of the day - some faux Italian concoction of pasta and vegetables. She settled on the latter on the grounds that it wouldn't require much chewing, thus making it easier to talk. She looked at her watch. Where was he? She could have done with glass of wine – or something stronger – but the café was unlicensed, so she ordered an orange juice, poured from a carton marked *Economy Catering Pack*.

* * *

Simon was making his way to the café when it began to rain. Damn. He'd forgotten his umbrella. He dodged beneath overhanging buildings to avoid the worst of it. The result was that he lost his bearings, found himself in the wrong street, and had to retrace his steps. All making him late.

Up ahead was the café. He could make out Alison through the café window as he closed in on it. He was pleased to see her, and hurried in.

'Sorry I'm late,' he said, as he reached the table. 'Long time no see.' He leant over and kissed her. She wiped her cheek 'Missed you,' he said as he sat down.

'Ooh, you're all wet,' she said, still wiping where he'd placed his kiss.

He pretended not to notice. 'Have you ordered?'

'Yes.'

'OK. I'll have one of those jacket potatoes. With cheese.'

He looked around for a waitress, thinking how tired Alison was looking. Unusually, she was wearing no makeup, and in the sombre light he had a sudden premonition of how she might look in fifteen or twenty years' time.

* * *

Simon was looking at his worst today, noted Alison. His hair was damp, flattened by the rain and plastered over his head most unbecomingly. His skin had a greyish hue and there was a drip at the end of his nose. Alison hoped it was rain and nothing worse. She had an almost unconquerable desire to seize her brown paper napkin – everything was brown in here – and wipe it off. She managed to resist.

Sometimes, she considered, Simon seemed more in need of a maid or valet than a wife. Whenever she stayed at his flat she would assume the role of a human vacuum cleaner; trailing in his wake and removing the mess and chaos he left behind.

Simon appeared to be peering around hopefully for a waiter.

27

'You have to order at the counter,' she said. 'Do you want me – '

'No. I'll do it. Back in a tick.' He backed out from his chair, narrowly avoiding a collision with someone coming in the opposite direction.

Alison sighed. If she could love him at his most hopeless and helpless, perhaps she ought to give him another chance. It wasn't as though he was all bad. He was capable of kindness and generosity and as men went, he was less selfish than many she'd encountered. Apart from off-days – like today – he was reasonably good-looking and, considering how little discernible effort he put into his career, was doing well at it. Not long ago he'd remarked quite casually that he would soon be in a position to pay off his mortgage. 'You could go a lot further and do a lot worse,' her mother had told her during one of their rare chats about Simon.

Simon returned, clutching a bottle of ginger beer. 'I haven't had any of this since I was about fourteen,' he announced, unscrewing the top and pouring it into a glass. Then he added: 'I meant it. About missing you. I'm sorry about what happened. Can we forget it and …well … if you want to move in, that's fine by me.'

Alison didn't say anything for a while. Sometimes, she realised, hope can be cruel, can tantalise. Trust him to ask now.

She sighed: 'Where is that going to get us?'

'I thought that's what you wanted.'

'I want a proper commitment.'

'But living together is a commitment.'

She stared at her empty glass. 'Not necessarily,' she said. 'I've known people who've lived together for years and … Well, and quite frankly Simon, I want to really settle down. And start a family. You see, I'm – ' and she was stopped, as the dish of the day arrived, and was plonked in front of her.

For some reason, she remembered that she'd never actually told Simon her age. Maybe he didn't realise how time was running out for her?

She thanked the waitress and tried again: 'The thing is, I feel that now is the right time for me. You know. To start a family.' How could she convey the longing, the desperation? Well, she'd said it now and there was no going back.

She waited for a response. He looked up from his drink. 'D'you know, I'd forgotten how sweet it was.' He smiled at her. 'And gassy too.'

'What?' she leant forward. Maybe she'd heard him wrong.

'The ginger beer.'

'I was talking about having children.'

'What? Honestly, Ali, I don't feel ready for anything like that. If ever I think about children, I think of them happening a long, long time into the future.'

She sat back and stared at him. 'You're thirty-six, Simon. You'd hardly be a young father as it is. You can't leave it forever.' Although she knew, of course, that wasn't strictly true. Men can have children whenever they want. It's so unfair.

'I'm not sure we could afford it anyway,' countered Simon.

'That's nonsense. Most people would have no trouble bringing up children on half your salary.'

'You don't know my salary,' he peered at her. 'Unless you've been peeking at my payslips. You haven't, have you?'

'Bloody charming.'

'C'mon,' he said. 'Let's enjoy lunch. Yours looks good. Don't wait for me,' he added, waving in the direction of her plate.

Alison picked up her fork her fork half-heartedly.

* * *

She's going to dump me. Any minute, Simon thought gloomily. That's the trouble with women. They keep on at you for months about something, then as soon as you give in, instead of being the slightest bit grateful or appreciative, they find something else to go on about. If I agree to a baby, it won't end there, oh no. Next thing you know she'll be insisting on a bigger house, bigger car, me giving up rugby …In his mind Simon saw the list of demands

29

stretching out into infinity. His jacket potato arrived, fresh out of the microwave, and his gloom deepened.

'That man over there looks like the Duke of Edinburgh,' he said, trying to lighten the mood.

'What man where?' She turned around. 'Oh. I suppose he does, in a way.'

It would be simpler if he didn't like Alison so much. He supposed he must love her – in a way. OK, she was self-opinionated, bit prissy at times about bed things, and infuriated him with her pernickety ways, but let's face it, he thought as he glanced at Alison across the table, she was interesting and part of his life, now. If she were to dump him, leaving him with just Petra – well, that would be like having all dessert and chocolate but with no main course. Petra was fun, great in bed. Fantastic tits. But he couldn't imagine living with her; they had nothing to talk about.

'Anyway,' Alison was saying. 'You're going to have to make your mind up. I'm not going to move in unless you do.'

A few tables away, a baby started to emit ear-splitting screams.

'Aren't we happy? Just the two of us?' said Simon. He had a sudden flash of a similar creature to the ear-splitter, waking him up all times of the night, demanding attention both ends (the needs of one of the ends he could not bear to speculate about).

* * *

Alison decided to try again. 'You'd soon get used to the idea of a baby,' she said. 'And, you'd make a great father.'

Alison's best friend Sally was of the opinion that Simon had lived by himself for so long that he was too used to having his own way. Doing what he wanted when he wanted.

'Look, he won't change unless he's forced to,' Sally had said.

'What do you mean?'

'If I were you, I'd get pregnant. Tell him it was an accident.'

'I couldn't do that. Besides, he wouldn't believe me.'

'Maybe not. But I know Simon. He'd do the decent thing and stick by you. He's a big softie at heart. Take it from me. He's not the type to demand you have an abortion.'

Simon's voice broke into her thoughts. 'I'm not sure I could cope with being tied down,' he was saying.

Alison placed her knife and fork and used napkin on her plate. She realised it was no good. She couldn't – no wouldn't – risk gambling her child's future that way. Her baby's father must want to be its father, not resent her child's very existence. She knew what she was going to do. Even if it meant putting her principles before her last chance of happiness.

'He'll come round in the end,' Sally's voice repeated in her head.

Alison shook her head, then regarded her boyfriend. 'You know what, Simon?'

'What, Al.'

'If you're not careful, you'll drift through life never committing yourself to anything or anyone. Is that what you really want?'

* * *

Simon looked down at his plate. His jacket potato was surrounded by a pool of rapidly congealing fat. He hated it when she started to hector him in that superior tone of voice.

'Maybe…one day…' he said.

'One day isn't good enough for me, Simon.' She stared at her watch. 'Ah well,' she said. 'Must go. I've got a meeting at two.'

She got up. 'I'll be over to collect my things in a day or so and I'll drop the keys through your letterbox.'

He looked up at her. 'So this is it,' he said.

'Yes. I think it's for the best.'

Gloom settled over him once more. He stood up. 'We'll still be friends, right?'

'I don't think so.' She collected her bag from under the table. 'A clean break will be better for both of us.'

Simon watched her walk across the brown, parquet floor. He wanted to call her back before she reached the door. He wanted to say: 'All right! Have it your own way! We'll get married and have half a dozen babies!'

But he didn't. Instead he sat back at the table as the door opened and closed behind her and she disappeared down the street beyond.

He picked up his glass and sniffed the contents. The froth on top of his ginger beer had all but disappeared, leaving a dirty brown sickly-smelling liquid. He put the glass down and pushed it away.

* * *

Alison walked purposefully in the direction of her office. For better or worse, it was done. She'd ring Mrs Jermyn this afternoon. Alison had no intention of returning to the dating scene. Leaving fate to its own devices was no longer an option; she'd decided to pick it up by the scruff of the neck, give it a good shaking, then push it very firmly in the right direction. Yes. She'd resolved to join a marriage bureau. Not a dating agency, but a good old-fashioned marriage bureau. OK, it charged a fortune, but at least there would be no misunderstanding about what she required – either by the proprietors or the clients.

Mrs Jermyn, the director, was a calm, authoritative woman, who assured her that women under forty were in great demand. And that, what's more, she could arrange at least a dozen suitable introductions. Alison told her that a slightly older man might do. Someone in his mid-forties perhaps. A widower would be ideal: maybe with one child already.

Mrs Jermyn had nodded. 'Entirely suitable,' she agreed.

When she got back to the office, Petra, the red-haired temp was there. On the phone, as usual. Smirking, Petra had announced that morning that she was pregnant. The office rumour was that she'd deliberately got pregnant so's her boyfriend would marry her. And no doubt he would, thought Alison. Petra was one of those women who always managed to get their own way in life. Well, good luck to her. Momentarily, she felt sorry for him. Whoever he was.

Caroline Ward

School photo

Here we sit
lined up neat as our cotton shoe bags.
Arms folded on desk tops
seamed by generations of compasses.
Girls' hair held by kirbygrips,
plastic clips and slipping ribbon;
hand-knitted cardigans buttoned in neat.
Boys' hair half way up their heads, severely damped
and wrenched to one side.
There's a smell of chalky board rubber,
shoe polish, warm milk bottles
and faintly, old wee.
All eyes front, because
Miss has eyes in the back of her head.

Outside
all the day is on tiptoe
looking through the window
and calling us.

Sarah O'Neill

The Queen who loved her bed

She couldn't get enough of the comfy stuff. Give her an eiderdown, no, three eiderdowns, all stuffed with feathers and embroidered with silk and taffeta, and then add some soft flannelette sheets of all colours, and then some real Scottish woollen blankets, some waffle ones and others thick and tartan and then some pillows, perhaps twenty on the bed, made of fur, suede, fluffiest feathers, softest mohair and cotton, all jumbled all over the bed, not just at the head, and the bed itself had to be huge and spacious enough for four people, because the Queen loved to have her beaus in bed or sometimes pyjama parties.

And she had a whole wardrobe full of bedwear. The fantastic Chinese robes and Indian kaftans, the woollen leggings worn by men, pure cotton long white nighties and sheer chiffon Playgirl stuff for the steamier nights.

Not that she liked to share the *whole* night with them, but she would toy with her lovers and then, when she was satisfied, she would send them back down the ladder – her bed was ten mattresses high – back to their tiny 3ft, cold, impersonal beds with their grey nylon sheets and itchy blankets, probably full of lice and other people's hair and bodily fluids dried on, in the furthest corner of the castle.

But *she* would sleep like a queen, because she *was* the Queen, and she loved her bed. She dozed a lot, but she made most of her decisions in her bed. She had pockets sewn into the top mattress, where she kept her supplies of chocolate and fine wine. Yes, up there she could really think and plan and make up the rules and she was totally on top of the world, and apart from the hoi polloi and she loved it in her fantastic bed and no-one could make her leave it unless she wanted to, and of course she had never married.

One day, the Queen asked for five thick duvets, fourteen fresh pillows, a box of rose petals and a packet of finest cigars. The ladies-in-waiting were quite used to her strange requests and fulfilled her wish, even though it was difficult for them to get it all up the ladder. The Queen did not move as they piled all the covers and pillows on top of her and scattered the petals like confetti over the top. Then they lit her cigar. The Queen demanded to be left alone, said quite firmly she was not to be disturbed, not until she beckoned them once more. And with that she sent them back to their cold benches beyond the heavy oak door.

Four days passed, then six. After ten days, they decided to enter her boudoir, on tip toes so as not to disturb her, and it was with shock that they found her, suffocated under the weight of the ton of bedding, with a smile on her face. Now she would never have to leave this room and this bed again, and it would forever be her bed of roses.

Ross Rossiter

Biannually

And the day will come
when you will find yourself
looking down the barrel
of an unloaded
Yale lock.
And you will think to yourself
"LORD, what have I done with my keys?"
And you will find yourself
searching your bedroom.
Searching the pockets
of the clothes
strewn
in your bedroom.
But you did not leave them there.
And you will think to yourself,
"They must be in the car."
And with a credit card
or suchlike
you will scrape the ice from the windscreen
and peer,
face cupped in hands,
nose against the frozen glass
and you will see
that you did not leave them there.
And you will think to yourself
"I was late for work ten minutes ago,
before I realised that my keys were lost."
And you will return to your domicile
and you will phone your boss
and you will explain
with reverence

your predicament.
You will replace the reciever
and relieved, you will sigh.
Your shoulders will drop,
and you will think to yourself
"I'm parched."
You will go to the kettle
and you will flick the switch
on the kettle
into
the 'on' position.
And you will go to the draining board,
and turn a mug
the right way up,
within which you will throw a teabag.
And you will go to the fridgidare
and pull open the door
(which weighs considerably less than the fridgidare door at your
mother's house)
and you will bend at the waist
and reach for the milk.
And lo,
malevolent,
a fob
with some keys
on the shelf
next to the milk,
and you will smile
and infuse the shredded leaves contained within the tiny bag
in freshly boiled water.
And you will milk your tea.
And you will smile some more
because you have the morning off work.
And the world is good.

Paul Roberts

Journey Home

I face forward and close my eyes as the plane lifts itself into the sky at an unlikely gradient. I crane to look back through the window, but in those seconds we have moved into cloud. There is nothing to see but the wings.

Slight turbulence shudders the plane within a minute of our being airborne. As it worsens, I exchange a nervous look with the man next to me. He raises his large eyebrows, and attempts a smile.

The light hurts my eyes when I look out now. We have emerged from the bulk of the cloud and are passing over billowing white monsters, hard-edged against the blue. After a while we level off, and the buffeting stops.

I relax a little and try to enjoy the show, try to picture the land, invisible beneath us. One of those map locators you get on long hauls would be nice, I think. I guess our position, and reckon we are above the empty moors and valleys of the southern uplands: ramshackle farms with sheep dogs and mud, empty lanes and rushing streams. Maybe we are above Hadrian's Wall.

I imagine the flight path will take us over the Eden valley and out across Kendal and Lancaster before heading down across northwest England and the midlands. Suddenly I am hit by nostalgia. It's as if flying over places I previously called home has stirred up forgotten memories.

The man next to me is speaking: 'I said, she wants to know if you'd like a drink.' He indicates to the stewardess who is leaning towards me.

I tell her no thanks, and as the man asks where my journey is taking me, I reply Bristol. Then I remember. I don't have my bag with me. Oh shit. It's back at the airport. I lose track of what the man is saying as I'm too busy uttering 'shit, shit, shit' under my breath.

'I beg your pardon,' says the man.

'Sorry,' I turn to him. 'I've just realised I left my bag behind. At the airport.'

I must have left it somewhere inside. I know I had it when I arrived in a cab to catch my plane. Jesus, what an idiot. And with all those announcements, as well, imploring people to keep their luggage with them at all times. I can't believe my stupidity.

Sheepishly, I ask the stewardess what I can do. She is sympathetic but explains the obvious: it is likely to have been removed for security reasons.

'Can you contact the airport?' She lets me down apologetically. Damn.

I go through what I had in it: a trashy novel I had just begun; my Walkman and tapes; a couple of work files; my personal journal; and, of course, Ellen's present. I always bring her something when I'm away for a night or more. She'll be expecting it. Damn. Now I'll be for it.

Of all the contents, it is the journal and the gift that really bother me. I hate to think that some stranger could be snooping into my personal thoughts. Worse still is the prospect of losing all the thoughts and impressions I had built up over the last few weeks. I was looking forward to sharing them with Ellen.

I feel powerless. If only I could do something. Ah well. There's nothing for it. Ellen will be there to meet me and I won't have anything to give her. Surely she'll understand. She knows how I feel without needing a present. She knows that I think about her when I'm away – doesn't she? But still I worry about that damn present.

For the rest of the flight I keep my head turned to the window even though my neck gets sore. The clouds have cleared and, as we fly lower, I can see fields, towns, and a busy road. I peer at these signs of human presence below me and, in an attempt to keep my mind from fretting about the bag, I try for ten minutes or so to determine where we are. Obviously approaching Bristol. Ah yes. There they are. The low Mendip hills and the village of Dundry. The sky is clear and the sun close to setting.

Inside Bristol Airport my case is one of the first off the carousel and, before I know it, I am heading through to arrivals when I spot her. She has already seen me and waves her left arm high above her head, smiling her wide smile. I walk up to her, and we hold each other close. For a moment.

'Hello you!' I say, pulling away.

'Have you missed me?'

'Yes of course.'

'I've missed you too.' She gives me a kiss then turns to go. I follow her through the sliding doors into the evening and the orange glow of the lowering sun.

'How was your flight?'

'OK, ' I lie.

Before long we are heading into town. The smell of the car air freshner she insists on having turns my stomach, and I wind the window down a fraction.

'And the trip?' she asks. 'How was that?'

'Good. Well, you know. Boring work stuff really.' It's hard to tell whether she's listening, so I leave it at that. I recognise that steeliness in her eyes as she negotiates the busy road. Her look is the one which suggests her mind is elsewhere. Why I haven't given her a present, perhaps. Normally I would have surprised her with her gift before now. For the time being, I decide to feign ignorance.

'I'd have liked to have seen more of Edinburgh,' I say. 'The lonely-man curry is about as much culture as I got.' She doesn't laugh at my attempt at humour. Instead, she flicks a look my way, and some stray curls fall across her forehead. She brushes them aside with her right hand. Her jerky, nervous movements give her a frightened animal quality which wrong-steps many people. Yet, if I'm honest, at the start, I'd found this rather attractive. Cute and vulnerable.

Finally, I say: 'You'll never guess. I left my bag at Edinburgh airport. There was something for you in it.'

'Jace,' she says, disbelief competing with amusement in her voice. 'You've lost your bag? How did you do that?'

'I think I left it on the floor at check-in. I expect they've picked it up. I hope. Don't know what I was thinking. Pre-flight nerves, I guess.'

'So,' she says. Eyes still on the road. 'What was in it?'

'Oh, the usual stuff. You know. My journal. And ... well, the worse thing is, Ell, I had something special for you. A lovely present. I'd searched high and low for it. Hopefully I can get a call through tonight and they'll be able to send my bag down. That is if they haven't blown it up or something. Thinking it's a bomb.'

We continue in silence then pull into a Texaco garage where Ellen gets out to fill the tank. I fully open the window, search my pockets for tobacco and papers, then roll a fag. When I'm done, I look up. Ellen is just walking in to pay. Across the forecourt a large billboard is advertising O_2 mobiles. Bubbles rise from a telephone to the top of the poster. Oxygen: the stuff of life.

I hold the roll-up in my lips, at first intending to wait until we are away from the pumps. Instead I close the window and light up with the in-built cigarette lighter. As we drive off I notice that someone has drawn smileys on some of the lower bubbles. I wonder whether to point them out to Ellen, but before I get a chance she starts in on Jan, continuing a telephone conversation we had begun last night.

Jan is Ellen's boss in the marketing company where she's worked for the last year. I met her at a function a couple of months ago. I took a particular interest in her because of Ellen's gripes.

She was taller than me, and had a way of talking and holding your eye far longer than necessary. Apart from that, she seemed perfectly nice. She told me about her husband's parents. They were starting a campaign in Southall to stop vandals from throwing rubbish into the Grand Union canal. I laughed, as I didn't think much of their likelihood of success. Jan had merely looked puzzled.

So, last night when I called Ellen from Edinburgh, she was telling me, as usual, what a bitch Jan was. Even now she is still telling me the ins and outs of an office life totally alien to me. Why can't Jan OK the training Ellen is so desperate for? Why does she keep her on the small ads? Why didn't Jan include her on the Ariston

41

project? And how can she, Ellen, possibly keep working with her? On and on she goes as I draw deeper on my cigarette and hope we return home soon. Clearly she's not expecting any response from me. And I realise that this is not the Ellen I fell for.

She is quiet for a while. Then, as we near the end of our road, she says: 'You just forgot didn't you?'

'Forgot what?'

'Admit it,' she says turning into our drive. 'You didn't get me anything, did you?'

I can't believe it. 'Don't be stupid. I told you, it was in my bag. And I left that at the airport.'

She pulls up outside our door and switches off the engine. 'So, come on then. What was it?'

I stare. 'It was going to be a surprise.'

She looks uneasy for a moment as though deciding whether to pursue this.

'I told you,' I say, all reasonable. 'All I have to do is call the airport and hopefully they'll be able to send the bag down to us. With your present.'

'Oh Jace! It's just. I don't know. I don't know whether I can trust you anymore. '

This takes me off guard. I am losing grip of what exactly she is talking about. 'Don't trust me?' I say.

'Well. Why won't you say what the present was.'

'I don't see why you can't trust me, Ell. I haven't done anything wrong. I can tell you what it is, but then it won't be a surprise anymore, will it?' I am beginning to lose my cool.

She searches for her bag and takes the keys out of the ignition. Clearly she is getting upset. 'I don't care anymore,' she says. 'The whole thing's ruined now anyway.'

She goes to open the car door.

'It's an alarm clock,' I say. 'I got you an alarm clock.'

'You got me an alarm clock,' she repeats the words flatly.

'Yes. A nice old style one. Chrome.'

We sit in silence for a while, and then I say: 'Come on, Ellen.

What's got into you?'

'Into me?'

'You're always unhappy, these days,' I say, knowing I'm fighting a losing battle. But I decide to stick with it. She stares straight ahead. 'D'you know what someone at the conference said to me yesterday?'

Still she says nothing.

"They said that fear is the cause of just about everybody's unhappiness in this country.'

She's looking over at me now. 'What are you talking about?' she says. Then: 'Oh, I give up.' She gets out of the car and slams her door. Words echo around inside the car like ghosts: incomplete and useless.

I walk into the house, but she's gone upstairs. So I pour myself a wine and decide to leave her to it. Next I reach for the phone and call Directory Enquiries for the Edinburgh airport number.

I am about to give up when a tired-sounding woman answers. She seems put out when I explain about my bag and ask to be put through to lost luggage or security. I am placed on hold for a few minutes. Greensleeves.

Come on. Come on. If I could I'd go back to the airport and pick up the bag myself.

A man, brisk and clipped, comes onto the line.

'You left your bag here?'

'Yes. This afternoon.'

'Can you describe it?'

'It's a black and blue backpack.'

'And where did you leave it?'

'I don't know. I was sat to the left of the main entrance for a while, just before the passport control area. I have a feeling it may be there.'

'Your name please?'

I give him my name, and the line goes blank for a moment. I am anticipating the arrangements for sending it here when a different man comes on.

'Mr Davis? Unfortunately we have been on heightened alert today, and this afternoon a bag fitting the description you gave was destroyed. I'm sorry. But we cannot afford to take any chances. I'm sure you understand.'

'But ...' Ellen comes out of the bedroom and sits halfway down the stairs. I hold the receiver away from my ear and look at her. My mouth opens but nothing will come out.

Paul Hilton

A Slow Night

Keith filled Morris Sheet's empty glass. Morris placed the required amount in fifty pence pieces on the counter.

'Ain't you got a note Morris? Thought you'd want to save your fifty p's for the meter.'

'Meter?' said Morris. He gulped a third of his drink then belched; his breath crossing the threshold of the bar and tweaking Keith's unfortunate nostrils.

'Cider. Sooner have that than lights,' he chuckled, then drank more.Keith passed him his change.

The clock on the wall behind Morris ticked loudly. It was ten minutes past ten. It's been a slow night, thought Keith, even for a Monday. Morris had been his only customer. A lorry rumbled past along the road outside, before the village fell silent again. Morris looked down at his broken arm as it lay in its yellowing sling. The cast now resembled a dirty stone, encasing his arm in a protective rock-hard shell. Morris, now adept at such a task, made a roll up with his one free hand. He'd told Keith that after the cast had been placed on, it was the first thing he'd learnt to do. A man cannot be reliant on another to make him a fag, he'd proclaimed.

'Slow night,' said Keith.

'Ah, tis.'

Keith pointed at the cast. 'When's that thing coming off then?'

'Presently.'

Keith leaned forward and adopted a conspiratorial stance. 'Go on, as there's just the two of us here. Tell us how you broke it.'

'I ain't broke it. Got a bruised bone is all. And no, I won't tell you.'

Keith sighed his mild frustration. He gazed at Morris, for despite Morris's bottomless pit of bad habits and his alarming ability to scare away anyone unfortunate enough not to be a regular, Keith held something resembling fondness towards him. He also appreciated

45

Morris's ability to drink everyday, for as long as Keith's pub was open. Should they introduce all-day licensing, Keith once remarked, during one of Morris's rare and noted absences from the snug bar of The Eagle, then Morris would not see his official retirement age – of which he was three years short.

'You don't want more accidents Morris. Not at your age.'

'Ah, hap-see jazz.'

'Those fifty p's. They won't keep your missus warm now will 'em?'

Morris fixed Keith with a stare that resembled some irksome Jack Russell. His eyebrows low on his face and his teeth hidden by a pair of tight chapped lips.

Keith knew this line of conversation – talking about his missus — would send Morris running to The Anchor Inn. Whilst Keith liked Morris, he sometimes despaired at his treatment of Mrs Sheet. She never frequented the pub, even at Christmas and New Year. When, about ten years ago, Keith had first bought and moved into the pub, he asked Morris when he might meet Mrs Sheet. Morris had merely stared back with that now familiar Jack Russell expression and then called Keith a stupid bastard. Keith barred him for that. But only for a week. In a village this size, you can't bar your regulars for just calling you a bastard.

Keith soon came to learn that for Morris, leaving his wife at home, sometimes with no lighting or heating, so that he could drink in the pub was more or less a conjugal right. Sometimes Keith would see Mrs Sheet walking to or from the shops, or to her daughter's, and she would seem a sad forlorn figure, who never spoke or smiled. Keith's wife had said: 'No bloody wonder the old dear looks sad. Married to that old sod.'

And it wasn't that Morris disliked the company of women. Far from it. A friend's wife would be 'a fine woman'. Young girls and daughters would be described as 'Angels from Heaven'. And Morris would refuse to sit if there was a woman standing in the bar. Occasionally, after twelve pints of cider – Morris's absolute limit (give or take the odd chaser) – he would intimate that he was

46

the victim of a broken heart. All Keith knew was that apparently this had happened during the war and that Morris's brief taste of romance had come to a sudden end. He'd heard it had something to do with a wayward German bomber pilot and a missed rendezvous at Chandler's hay barn. Unfortunately, what with Morris being so inebriated on the rare occasions he mentioned it, no one could make out what he was saying, and the next day Morris would avoid all mention of the subject. All that was clear were the tears that would well up in the corner of his green eyes on the nights when he was pissed and remembering.

Morris finished his drink and opened the bag of pork scratchings that lay next to his glass. After he finished he asked for another pint of cider. 'And a whisky.'

'Scotch?' said Keith, somewhat thrown, as it was unlike Morris to drink spirits. Unless the occasion demanded it. Christmas, New Year, his birthday, his daughter's birthday, Easter and the birthday of his grandchildren. Come to that, the birth of any child whose parents he may have some acquaintance with. And English sporting triumphs were another reason to waft the grain under his red pointed nose. However, an uncalled-for chaser on such an ordinary Monday, not even a Bank Holiday, was practically unheard of.

Morris nodded yes to the scotch, and licked the remains of his snack from his lips. He then sucked the salt from his fingers. They made a popping sound as his small, greedy mouth let them go from his chapped lips, wet digit by wet digit.

Keith poured his usual measly measure of whisky. It had taken him a number of years of experimentation with various dispensers to perfect this. Keith had proudly told his wife that his measures were possibly one eighth under the standard. No one ever noticed and he counted his yearly savings in ten and twenty pound notes.

Morris plonked down sixty pence in five pence pieces and assorted coppers. Keith feared for the grandchildren's piggy banks. Morris stared at his glass in silence as the clock ticked some more.

The outside door opened in the saloon on the other side of the bar. Morris craned his neck to look past Keith. Andy Haynes, Derek

Haynes's son, had come in with someone Keith didn't recognise. As a greeting, Morris produced his unfriendly canine stare. Keith went through to the other side of the bar to serve them. The two men ordered lager, much to Morris's obvious and snorted disgust.

'Who's that with Derek Haynes's boy?' Morris asked when Keith returned.

'He's with that couple that moved into the bungalow, opposite Colin Billings.'

'The one with that pond in the front?'

'That's he.'

Morris squinted at the youth pondering over the jukebox.

'I don't like the look of he.'

'I doubt he likes the look of you much.'

Morris laughed. The clunk of the jukebox, rising from its Monday night slumber with the strains of 'Smoke on the Water' and the clack of billiard balls, stopped Morris short. He'd made it clear on several occasions that he didn't approve of Keith's recent attempts to widen The Eagle's appeal. The saloon bar should have been kept as it were – he'd tell anyone who'd care to hear – somewhere to stack chairs and to sleep a lunchtime session off.

'Fucking rubbish music. I'm going down The Anchor if this keeps up.'

Keith smiled at the empty threat. 'You're barred,' he said. 'Peggy told me.'

'I ain't barred.'

'You are. You kicked their cat.'

Morris gave a wry smile.

'Fucking thing that was. I didn't think it would go that far.'

Keith laughed, despite himself – because no-one likes cruelty to animals, do they?

'Ah well,' he said. 'Peggy reckons the cat's alright now.'

'I'd better get back up there then, and finish the bastard off.'

Keith had heard the stories about Morris's cruelty to animals. Like most of his generation thereabouts Morris had worked on one of the farms that surrounded the village. Yet, despite this rural upbringing, Morris had apparently shown little inclination towards Nature, and even less so towards working with it. On his arrival in the village Keith had been introduced to Morris via a series of stories that often involved an altercation with some unfortunate creature. Weston-super-Mare donkeys and farm dogs in particular would fare badly upon even the briefest contact with Morris.

It was claimed he'd lost a farmhand job after he'd stolen a lamb from Ken Masters. This had only been discovered after a botched kitchen slaying had left the previously sweet bundle of wool running through the neighbours gardens, blood gushing from a torn throat as it fled from Morris, the amateur slaughter man, waving his wife's bread knife in his hand. Young children that witnessed the event were still disturbed by the images, years later, one of the regulars had whispered. In the end a neighbour had finished it off and cursed Morris, who had simply offered to buy him a drink.

Family pets that sniffed at his overgrown hedgerow, or dared to cock a leg at the green weeds and yellow dandelion flowers received whatever Morris had to hand, flung at them with exceptional venom and, for such an habitual drinker, some accuracy. Although never proved, the disappearance of his daughter's pet rabbit 'Snowy' had coincided with a dish of lapin a la frites at the Baber household. Or so they say.

Morris could often be heard spouting off in the pub about how he believed that all kindness to animals was sentimental. And Keith had heard that he also applied a similar logic to his dealings with any child over five. Whilst somehow managing to produce a daughter with what Keith could only imagine was the unwilling assistance of Mrs Sheet and now himself a grandfather, Morris would take what appeared to be great pleasure in cuffing neighbours' children around the head for any perceived misdemeanour. Such crimes against Morris would include playing too loudly, laughter, running, skidding bicycle wheels, and - for reasons only known to him – playing a game of cricket.

Morris was not unknown to the police, after upset parents had reported him, but despite some harsh words, Morris continued in his wide-ranging vendetta, striking fear into any child or teenager that crossed his path.

Morris finished his whisky and got off his stool.

'Night then,' said Keith.

'Ah,' was all Morris said. And he walked out into the night air, leaving the clock on the wall ticking as the door closed behind him.

* * *

Keith heard the news the following morning; and to his surprise his immediate reaction was one of guilt, followed quickly by a surprisingly deep pang of sorrow.

He was standing in the street pointlessly supervising the brewery's weekly delivery when Jane Phelps crossed the street and told him what had happened. Morris had collapsed on his way home and been found by his son in law, Terry. Mrs Sheet had wandered down to her daughter's to ask them to look for him as he'd not returned from The Eagle. She couldn't ring anyone herself, as Morris hated the telephone and refused to contemplate one in his household. Even in a crisis, it seemed that Morris's foibles were a burden to his wife.

He was found close to home, just around the corner from their semi-detached council house, lying alongside Tim Benjamin's yellow, souped-up Ford Cortina. A car Morris openly detested.

At first, Terry had thought Morris was drunk. He'd stood there, berating him for having had too much to drink – assuming that he had passed out and was now asleep on the pavement. Well, it wouldn't have been the first time. Apparently it wasn't until Terry prodded his father in law that he realised something more serious had happened. The ambulance he called turned out to be a formality. Morris was already dead from a heart attack.

* * *

A week later, Keith attended the funeral. He didn't sit by the Sheet family – he was feeling too bad. He studied the scene and was genuinely surprised at the turnout. A number of people who had refused to talk to Morris for years were there amongst his friends. Keith couldn't shake his feeling of guilt. He couldn't escape the fact that Morris had died before his time because of drink, because of drink which Keith had sold him.

No-one said anything to him, but nodded when they caught his eye. Morris's daughter thanked him for coming.

The wake was held at the daughter's house, but Keith didn't go. Instead he returned to The Eagle and opened up for a few of the regulars. They drank a formal toast and swapped a number of Morris-related stories. Some made Keith laugh so hard that tears filled his eyes. Most of them ended with Morris falling off a barstool, or getting smacked off one. The stories made Keith feel easier as it seemed Morris had drunk heavily in whatever pub he was in and would have always done so. Keith almost felt a little pride that such a serial drunk spent his last days happily in the pub he owned.

After last orders the regulars filed out, and Keith waved them goodbye. He allowed himself a moment to stand alone, with just the ticking clock for company.

Slowly he cleared up. Mopping the floors and emptying the ashtrays. He walked to the back of the bar to put the glasses in the washer, enjoying the silence of the empty room. He wondered if he should stay closed, out of respect. It was a Wednesday, after all, and Wednesday nights could be slow. There again, he thought, maybe closing the pub wasn't the most appropriate way to mark Morris's passing.

Then, to his annoyance, Keith heard the door of the snug bar open. He wiped his hands on a tea towel and walked back out to the bar to explain that he was closed. Instead he said: 'Hello Mrs. Sheet. And what can I do for you?'

Mrs Sheet stood in the middle of the room gazing around at the nicotine-stained wallpaper and old brewery posters. She was a little taller than Morris, Keith noticed. She was dressed in a grey skirt and a black top. Her grey hair tightly held back by a black ribbon. Keith found it difficult to focus on her face, as it seemed dominated by the enormous national health glasses she wore. Her magnified eyes blinked at him. She said something, but her voice was timid and quiet and the words barely audible. Keith couldn't catch what she said and apologised.

'Where did he sit?' she repeated.

'Sit?' Keith smiled at her. 'Just there.' And he pointed to Morris's stool at the bar. Mrs Sheet walked over to the stool and, to Keith's surprise, climbed onto it and sat down. She continued to look around, taking in the view Morris had known for so many years.

'Can I get you a drink, Mrs Sheet?'

She scrunched up her nose and looked a little embarrassed.

'On me. I feel I owe you one.'

'What would he have?' her little voice asked.

'Well, he'd drink cider. That was his usual'

She scrunched up her nose again. 'Don't like that.'

'You can have a soft drink, if you'd rather.' There was a pause as she thought. 'Tell you what,' said Keith. 'He liked a whisky as well. Will you have one with me?'

She nodded. He filled two glasses with double measures and the two of them sat in silence. She sipped her whisky, occasionally wincing at the taste, but refused any water or mixer.

Keith had to ask: 'If you don't mind, Mrs Sheet. Can I ask, how did Morris break his arm? Only, he wouldn't tell us, see.'

'Caught him with his hand in my purse. Whacked him with the poker.'

Keith's lips wobbled slightly as he fought hard to keep his solemn expression from turning into a smile.

Mrs Sheet continued to stare to the side of him, at the wall of spirits and photographs that surrounded the till.

After a few minutes she finished her drink. 'Thank you,' she said.

'My pleasure, Mrs Sheet. Come back anytime.' But she merely

scrunched up her nose once more, and walked out.

Keith got up and locked the door behind her. He sat back on his side of the bar and lit a cigarette. He finished his whisky to the sound of the clock, ticking loudly on the wall.

Judy Green

Ephemeral Memorial

Something met its end here,
soft white hairs mark the spot.
Amongst fragile crocuses,
that edge the empty green,
something struggled and lost.
Next to the joggers' highway,
pock-marked by studs and horses' hooves,
cloud-wispy down bears witness,
forlorn evidence of a life lived precariously.
                    It will soon drift and be dispersed,
perfect material for nesting birds,
whose clear notes mingle in a requiem,
above the noise of passing cars.

Alex Maxwell

Bully Boy

Ding – dong! Oh thank god.It's the cavalry. Next door has heard the Sunday lunch hit the kitchen wall and has come to save me.

'Who the fuck…?'

His hand is still raised as I am crouched down by the fridge. Responding to the doorbell, he goes off down the hall to present that sane, charming neighbour face he has for the outside world. I relax, but only for a moment. It's not safe yet. Then, as if he can hear me thinking about moving, his voice comes back. 'Don't think about going anywhere, Kate, we're not finished with this.' And I hear him open the door.

But I am finished. I am so finished. This must be the end. Yet I can't see how. Voices drift down the hall. Someone is polling for the local Conservative Party. Carefully, I ease up onto my knees. He'll be ages. He loves a good old political rant. Loves to think he's got the better of people – one way or another.

'And so,' I hear from the doorway. 'If I could ask sir, will we be able to count on your support at the general election?'

'I've always supported what is best economically for myself and my country, but I'm not entirely sure if I agree one hundred percent with what the current Chancellor has done….'

Patronising, pompous bastard, I think. I tune the conversation out and stare listlessly at the spaghetti bolognaise oozing down the wall above the cooker. I know I should clean it up, my supposed slovenly housekeeping being one of his biggest bugbears. Instead I just watch the congealed mess and wonder how I'm going to escape from the hideous tangle that has ended up being my life.

He'd always been arrogant, but I was naïve and eager for life to begin, and so I didn't notice. I'd thought a flash car and a good career in insurance was a great deal. Let's face it, anything would have been a good deal when it offered the chance to get away from the net curtains and the chintz covers, the hidden gin bottles and the maudlin crying jags of my lonely, drunken mother.

'But, darling, you can't marry him, he's a salesman, for goodness sake. Why on earth would you want to waste your time with him? You're young. You've got your whole life before you. You don't need to think about marrying yet.'

'Please stop going on and on, Mummy. I'm going to marry him, he's asked and...'

'Oh Christ! You're not pregnant are you?'

'I'm twenty-two, Mum, and it's the nineteen eighties. Would it really matter if I was? Apart from how ashamed you'd be of me marrying someone you consider beneath us, of course.'

I can still remember how hard my heart had thundered when I defied her to marry my man. But it wasn't anywhere near as hard as my heart had hammered the first time he hit me. And now it's happened so many times I can't even remember what threw his switch that day. Only that it had come from nowhere. Signet ring stinging my ear, my head bouncing back off the door frame.

That last time I saw my mother in her overstuffed sitting room, her face all blotched red and face-powder white, her mascara making two scrawled black lines down her cheeks, she'd pawed my hands clammily, her sweet gin-breath in my face: 'Darling, please, please think again. Don't marry him. Don't go with him. Stay with me please, darling. I need you. I can't be alone, I...'

And I couldn't get away fast enough. I'd welcomed him with open arms. And then it had taken years of snide comments and put-downs about my looks, my intelligence, my abilities as a wife, before my euphoria at escaping had dampened. And now look – I needed to escape again.

I am literally jerked out of my reverie by the hand tangled in my hair hauling my head up. I try to stay down by the fridge, trying to make myself as small as I can, to disappear like a snail. Only I don't have a shell. He's standing over me, fist clenched, his rage rising off him like heat haze off a car bonnet.

'What the fuck are you doing, sitting there on your lazy arse? Didn't I tell you to bloody well make me something decent for my lunch?'

He drags me by my hair into the hall and opens the door to the cupboard under the stairs. I start to whimper.

'Filthy cow Kate. You should have cleaned that foreign shit off my kitchen walls by now.'

I grab hold of the doorframe to try and stop him, but he is pushing me into the dark.

'Please, please don't put me in there. I'll clean it up, ' I sob. I hate him so much for making me beg.

He continues as if I haven't spoken, in fact I expect he didn't even hear me, miles away in his own righteous world.

'I don't work as hard as I do to have to live in a pig sty, woman. I keep you, so the least you can do is look after me the way I want.' The door slams and the bolt is shot. I am alone.

I want to shriek, I want to pound on the door with my fists, but I am too frightened. Once, early on, I did exactly that and he opened the door and flung a kettle of boiling water over me. That he must have actually stood and patiently waited for the kettle to boil, while I banged on the door for him to let me out, is nearly as frightening to me now as was the peeling burn on my neck. Laura had noticed it and asked if I'd had an accident.

'Oh no, I split some tea. Stupid really.'

'You spilt it on your neck?' she said, staring at me. 'Are you crazy? Did Colin do it?'

'It was an accident, Laura, honestly,' I'd said, turning away. 'It's nothing. He just tripped and accidentally scalded me with his tea.' That was the closest I'd ever come to talking to anyone about it. And I blew it. Pathetic.

Recently I've thought about smothering him, or poisoning him, or I could stab him with a knife. I've thought about simply leaving, but the enormity of going anywhere and explaining why a person would let themselves be tormented and beaten for ten years without doing anything about it defeats me.

I imagine what Laura might say: 'Just leave. Leave him and come stay with us.'

'But I haven't any money,' is what I imagine I'd say back. 'And I'm not qualified to do anything.'

'You could learn. Hundreds of people do. Hundreds of women leave every day.'

'But I can't,' I always find myself saying, as I know it's true. 'He'll find me. Because if I run away, then everyone would know what he'd done. And he'd never stand for that. So he'd find me … and …'

I imagine her face, her disappointment in me. The thought that, it can't really be that bad if I can't bring myself to leave; that I must be making it up. She wouldn't, couldn't, understand how soul-destroying it is — how confidence-sapping, how terrifying – the thought of people whispering behind their hands that I must have done something to deserve it.

I rub my forehead back and forth over the rough wood of the cupboard door as if this might conjure up a genie who will grant me three wishes. For him to be dead, for him to be dead, for him to be dead.

I guess that he must have gone out, now. It's quiet and I can't hear the sound of the television. He usually spends Sunday afternoons getting furious watching the sport which then usually ends up with me getting a bruise or two.

Eyes wide in the dark, and with my arms outstretched, I feel my way to the back of the cupboard; there are his golf clubs, the cat basket, his tool kit. I feel along the edge of the box, praying its not locked. It isn't. It opens.

'Thank you, genie, thank you,' I whisper under my breath into the stuffy darkness; as if my wishes really have been granted. My hand has closed on a chisel, and a little voice in my head says: 'What on earth do you think you are going to do with that? You won't be able to kill him with that. And anyway, even if you do. How is a life sentence better than this?' Outside, a door slams, and I can hear him coming.

Shit, oh shit, I think. Can I do this? Then the voice comes: 'How can I not?'

The bolt grinds back, and the door opens. Eyes scrunched to the light, my arm is grabbed as he drags me out. With all my might, with the full weight of my despair and anger, I stab him in the thigh with the chisel and, as he yells and crashes to his knees, again in the neck. It's not enough, I know it isn't. But finally I am lucky. He falls headfirst into the cupboard. Before he can move I shove his legs in and slam the door and bolt shut.

'Kate, Kate you fucking bitch,' he is screaming. 'When I get out of here I'm going to strip your skin off. I'm going to break your fucking legs.' The door practically bursts off its hinges with the fury of his kicks.

My mouth is open and I am panting like a dog shut in a summer car. I can't stop to think now. I heave the sideboard, that hideous, heavy, mahogany wedding present from his hideous, heavy, wooden mother, in front of the door. Then without a backward glance, I walk into the kitchen.

'Kate,' I can still hear coming from under the stairs. 'What are you doing, you bitch? Why are you doing this to me? Kate, Kate. Come on, darling. Come back. Let me out. I'm … I'm sorry Kate. Really, I can't help it. I do love you, I don't mean it, Kate.' Door rattles. 'Kate! Come here, Kate. Now! Kate! Fuck you, Kate, you cow …'

The lunch continues its slide down the tasteful cream tiles, and I wonder how long it takes for someone to die of thirst and blood loss, and what I might do with the body. How can I explain where he has gone? What if next door hears him? But they have never heard him breaking my arm or beating me with a golf club so why should they notice this? He sounds fainter already. No-one sees much of me anyway, I think. Because I always have to wait for the bruises to fade, don't I? So no-one will notice if I'm not here. I could leave right now.

The insane relief of not having him breathing next to me, of having that threatening glowering presence safely locked away, makes me laugh. I don't think about the consequences, or the police. I just laugh and laugh. Tears running down my face.

Alison Chlebik

Every Little Thing

From the window she can see the whole garden. Her eyes follow the line of the fence. One of its wooden panels had come loose, blown forward in the wind, leaving a gap just big enough to climb through. It's fixed now, and properly upright: a good, strong line with no weakness. Her eyes move round to the gate, checking it's closed tightly, the silver latch in its proper place. It's a good, quiet neighbourhood. But you never know who's about.

She looks at the little figure on the lawn, then smiles at his stripey, red hat, its bobble wobbling as he bends down. She watches Danny grab a handful of grass, stand up, then stretch his arm out to view his fist full of spikey green. He's running, then stops and turns quickly on the spot. She starts forward, close at the window: sees the fall, feels the pain. But Danny is smiling, spinning safely. Little blades fall through his fingers, floating, feather-landing on the lawn. She steps back, hand on chest, her breath a mist on the glass. And now he is still, looking down at his red boots. She can see they're shiny-wet and knows she was right to insist he wear them. His coat is zipped up to his chin – what mother would have it otherwise, when even such a bright day can quickly turn cold at this time of year?

Red boots are jumping. She hears rubbery landings through the glass. When they first moved here there had been a pond over there, in the corner, beyond the path. Shaded by evergreen laurels the water was a dark mirror, its edge hidden in long grass and weeds. She had been assured that the depth was shallow, the algae harmless, but who could trust such liquid shadows? The pond filled and made into a rockery within a week of their moving in. Now it is bright with purple and yellow pansies, sweet with the scent of blue and white hyacinths nearby. The sun on the window catches the colours, trapping them in rainbow smears.

Beyond the glass she sees Danny jumping to the rockery's

60

edge, then stoop and pick up something from between the flowers. Something brown: mud or a stone maybe. He rubs it with his fingers, then puts it to his face, holding it under his nose. Her hand goes to the curtain, eyes fixed on the little face, an earthy taste already on her tongue. The boy drops the stone. She smiles: hasn't she told him about germs, warned him not to put things in his mouth? One day she will explain about busy roads and wicked strangers. When she calls him indoors they will wash his hands together.

The stripey, red hat bobs on the path beneath the window. Danny stops, watching a bird on the lawn, his face fixed, arms out as wings at his sides. He is so close. She waves, but Danny doesn't see. She taps on the glass. He jumps; looks around in alarm. She sees the little figure trembling, the startled bird soar away.

"It's alright, Danny!" She is at the door. The handle sticks, her hand fumbles. "Don't be frightened. I'm coming. No, don't cry."

Clare Harris

Valentine's Day 2004

I dream an ancient dream
of half-heard harsh voices muttering vengeance,
tribal loyalties calling;
Boudicaa's warriors stream Iceni blue
against the purple Eagle;
arrows rain futile on clashing armour,
horses scream,
fires rage in a dark beech forest;
a King's death is avenged.
I dream an ancient dream.

With cock crow, my mouth stings
with bitter herbs and ashes;
I cannot stand up straight.
Eyes full of bitter tears,
I cannot stand up straight.

Rolling Pin

Blunt-headed, water-stained wood,
two foot long, four inches round,
rolling in big knuckled, red,
flour-covered hands.
Apple scent fills the kitchen.

Kate Gardiner

I Can See My House From Here

He was always finding an excuse to walk past her house. The relationship had ended badly but he hoped he would bump into her, even though it was often very late at night, or in the early hours, when he walked by. He would drag his feet, stop to light a cigarette, or fumble with change in his pocket. Sometimes he imagined he had dropped his keys, and would re-trace his steps, ready with an excuse should she catch him. He only lived a few streets away. He knew that he could see the roof of his house if he stood on the end of her bed. He had tried it once and the thought of it made him feel safe.

His friend Ashley lived a couple of streets further up and he walked past her house when he went to visit. There were lots of other reasons he found for being in her road. He put his name on the allotment waiting list and would routinely go and check if he was any nearer the top. He walked to the local café and took the scenic route there. He considered getting a dog just so he could take it for walks in the park next to the allotments. Wake up and smell the coffee, Ashley had said after the first time she had tried to end it. She's not interested, mate, you've got to move on. He had wanted to punch Ashley then.

The For Sale sign appeared without warning and shocked him. He wondered why she wanted to sell when she had been so resistant to his suggestion that she move in with him. It was only practical, he had argued, he had so much more space, had even been prepared to convert the garage into a studio for her. The thought that she had met someone else and was on the verge of moving in with him, or worse, moving away, itched painfully at his skin. The lack of knowing made him feel angry, it was typically wilful of her somehow. He had not given up hope, entirely, that one day, despite the acrimony, they would get back together again. The bold lettering and gaudy colours of the For Sale sign mocked him.

He walked briskly up the path. It was lunchtime and she was

unlikely to be there but he took the precaution of ringing the bell. When there was no response he crouched down and flicked open the letterbox. The usual view through the hall and into the kitchen was obscured by some kind of bristly backdrop, a new fixture, he noted. He stood there for a few seconds, looking hard at the door, willing it to open, forgetting momentarily that they had agreed it was best for them not be in contact for a while. She didn't like people to call round unexpectedly. He remembered the time he'd turned up at six in the morning with fresh croissants and coffee. But if you love someone you're happy to see them any time aren't you, he'd asked, bemused. That was one of the things she used to complain about, he never gave her enough space, tried too hard to control things. She could be rude like that, scornful even, but he found it exciting.

From Ashley's house he called the estate agent and arranged a viewing for later that afternoon. Ashley fixed a pot of tea and tried to persuade him against it. What do you hope to gain, he asked, exasperated. Then, more gently, isn't it a bit weird? Ashley offered to come with him, but he wanted to go alone. They were both freelancers and worked from home. Ashley had only recently given him a lecture on the dangers of enforced solitude, urging him to go mountain biking or snow boarding with him.

He couldn't explain why he needed to go or what he hoped would come out of it. Perhaps she was in trouble and needed his help, or perhaps the sign had gone up outside the wrong house. He would leave her a note, asking her to give it just one more try, and she would come running back. Maybe this was what she had in mind when she put the house up for sale, knowing he would see the sign.

He felt suspicious of the agent who met him outside the house, his predictable self-tan and goofy smile irritated him. Despite this he tried to imagine what a genuine house purchaser might do or say, nice view, he offered feebly in the sitting room. Little had changed, it was scattered with her and the sight and scent of it all made him weak. He followed the agent around forlornly. As you will see, the vendor's really done some work here, you could move in, unpack a bag and be quite happy here. He had been instrumental in many of the improvements the agent referred to, had re-furbished the kitchen and helped her paint the front room. Together they had gone to salvage yards, found old pine doors which he'd stripped and restored. She had seemed incapable, somehow, of sorting out practical things, although she had a good sense of colour. He had enjoyed fixing things for her, putting up a shelf or mending the garden fence. She was highly-strung and artistic, over educated, he had called her once, with no common sense. Rather that than the other way round, she replied, tartly. That was her all over, quick and witty, it made him giddy just to think of it. The vendor has been rather clever, said the agent, in just a few years this property has almost doubled in value and with the funky, yet cosy feel, it's bound to get snapped up. He winced at the agent's patter.

Do you know why she's selling, he asked, wishing he had the strength to build more of a rapport with the agent, who might conceivably share more information than was strictly professional. Moving somewhere bigger, I believe, said the agent, vaguely. Local, he asked? Not sure, replied the agent, leading the way out to the back garden and gesturing, with a wave of his hand, towards the apple tree he had planted for her. He wondered if she had flirted with the agent, imagined her showing him around, offering him a cup of tea, something fancy like lemon and ginger, or raspberry. Love to try it, the agent would have said, although really being the kind of guy who never strayed from instant coffee. The garden brought back even more memories of their time together. He had wanted to make her happy and believing he couldn't compete intellectually had tried to make himself useful, in practical ways, and with gifts and treats. She was always saying she was skint and so he had taken her on holiday and bought her things. He thought she was the kind of woman who ought not to be shopping in charity shops even though she claimed to enjoy it. He couldn't understand that. Didn't all women want a man to buy them nice things, women like his ex wife, in fact every woman he had ever dated.

They came back into the house and went up the stairs. Typically she had left the window open in her bedroom, oblivious to the risk of burglars, and a slight breeze tugged at the curtains. He became aware that every bone and muscle in his body ached and he felt an overwhelming urge to crawl into her bed and sleep for a very long time. He wondered if he wasn't well, perhaps Ashley was right, he'd been spending too much time on his own. He felt a slight swell of seasickness and struggled to focus on the moment. The agent was motioning outside of the bedroom towards a hatch in the ceiling and the attic space above. Yes I'd like to see the attic, he said, and watched silently as the agent pulled the internal ladder down. I'm thinking of a loft conversion, he added, feeling ridiculous.

He had never been in the attic before, had only vaguely been aware of its existence. There is a light up there, the agent shouted from below, and he groped in the dark for its pull. A murky 40-watt lit the rafters. He couldn't stand to his full height but crouched and scuffed along to the furthest point where a crack of light showed between the roof tiles. He craned his neck and peeked through. He worked his way along the backs of houses in his street until, finally, he found his house and realised he was looking in to his own bedroom. Hey, he shouted down to the agent, I can see my house from here. He saw his life in miniature then and imagined himself as a giant plunging an enormous hand through the roof tiles, reaching out over the house tops and tree tops and wrenching his own house completely from its foundations, before stomping off with it over the city and into a brave new future. Trouble was, he didn't feel big or courageous, he felt small and daft. What would anyone think if they knew what he'd done? What would she say if she came home right at this moment? He stood up sharply, banging his head on a beam, and resisted the urge to sit down and weep. He stepped sheepishly down the ladder and stood before the agent, brushing the dust off his clothes.

Cheers mate, he said, thanks, I've seen enough now. He hurried down the main stairs, not waiting for the agent. If you'd like to book a second viewing at any time just let me know, he heard the agent's voice behind him. He strode purposefully towards the front door just as her ginger tom came out from the sitting room, meowing and yawning. He'd never liked the cat it was fickle and mercenary. He took a petulant booted swipe, missed, and was rewarded with a vicious hiss and a malevolent stare. Have a think about it, the agent called, relentless, as he stepped out into the fresh air. He turned, reluctant to shake the agent's hand, but wanting an ending, something affirmative. The agent's hand was warm and damp, but he gripped it hard. You can always tell a man by his handshake his father used to say. I've decided it's not really what I'm after, he said, firmly, but thanks anyway. He turned then, in a hurry, eager to complete the short distance home.

Ginetta Martinez

Duggie's New Coat

The usual ads rolled by as I was shunted along the bowels of London underground. Headed for Oxford Circus with styrofoam cup of coffee in one hand, violin case in the other. From where I sat, I stared at the before and after pictures for cosmetic surgery, chat lines for the sad and lonely, and the latest Hollywood bollocks – sorry, "films". Oh yeah, and "Les Mis". That's what my girlfriend Sonia calls it. "Les bloody Mis". Not that I see her much, she's always rehearsing for the stupid musical. But when I do it's "Les Mis" this, and "Les Mis" that.

Last night she rang to say they were starting early this morning so she was going to spend the night with a friend who had a flat near the theatre. *Again.* Third time this week. The only colleagues I have who live close to work sleep in doorways. And when she's not rehearsing she's shopping – she used to *hate* shopping. And when she's not shopping she's drinking with her cronies.

There was a new ad in my usual busking spot. Wonderbra. A half-naked chick with the words 'Hello boys' underneath. Someone had written in big red letters, 'THIS ADVERT IS AN INCITEMENT TO RAPE:' On the other hand I thought, as I got out my violin and stroked rosin along the strings, it might hopefully incite large donations to unemployed musicians if it stops commuters in their tracks. Better than the ad that was there before. Nationwide Building Society. I mean. That was just going to remind people they've got a mortgage to pay and shouldn't be wasting their hard-earned on some loser who's only one step up from a beggar and ought to get on his bike and get a proper job like everyone else.

It was cold. I was grateful for my new coat. Well, new from the charity shop, that is. Sonia had picked it for me.

I launched into the theme from 'Titanic' Paganini's more my style. And Mozart. He's the king. But your average Oxford Circus punter is *not* interested in Paganini. South Ken, yeah. Holborn

68

maybe. But not Oxford Circus. Plebs, the lot of them. They want your 'Bridge over Troubled Water', don't they? And bloody, 'Michelle, Ma Belle'. And of course, *anything* by that bastard Lloyd Webber. So I give the punters what they want. Just don't blame me if one day I crack, and go round and shoot Andrew Lloyd Webber.

So, that day, I played 'Titanic' so schmaltzy you could almost hear the screams, and feel the icy water round your ankles – till, that is, I was drowned out by the rumbling of trains, screeching brakes and computer-generated announcements to 'STAND CLEAR OF THE DOORS.' Each time the doors open you have to brace yourself as this foul rush of bacteria-sodden air precedes the crowd as they push their way through and out towards the escalators. Sometimes you're all ready, poised for the crush, and just one solitary person trundles out looking confused and embarrassed, like they've suddenly found themselves alone on a big stage. That's when I like to break into 'The Halleluiah Chorus.'

Anyway a lonely pile of coins was gathering at my feet. 'And the band played on, mate!' I shouted after one po-faced bastard who'd bloody thrown his sandwich wrapper into my case. Still, I have to watch it. Keep the punters sweet. I'm still paying my fine. Two thousand pounds, five pounds a week – they'll have to dig me up for the rest.

Suddenly I could sense someone watching me. I looked around and there he was. Smiling at me. Kind of smug, like he knew something I didn't. He was smooth. Mediterranean-looking, with longish dark hair. Stood in front of the tube map with a cello in one hand and a book in the other. Maybe I knew him from somewhere. College? Or maybe he was after this pitch. Maybe he didn't know about the unspoken rule. (There's this unspoken rule, see, that says you have to move on after two hours to let someone else use the pitch. Busking etiquette, right?) Well, he was just going to have to wait. My two hours weren't up. Usually I move on to the South Ken tunnel after this session. You can play classical stuff in South Ken. Better class of punter, see?

69

Anyway, this guy didn't look like a busker, what with his smart blue coat. So, what the hell did he want? He could be the personnel officer for the London Philharmonic on the lookout for talent (though I don't suppose he'd be looking in the underground – would he?). I was beginning to suspect he was on the lookout for a different kind of talent. Look. Not that I mind. I'm not the sort who's going to punch some poor bloke just 'cause he fancies me. No mate, I'm flattered. But I like women. That's all. Ask Sonia. Anyway, I didn't look across too much in case I gave him the wrong idea. It's the coat, I thought. My new coat makes me look so damned hunky.

I decided to play "Don't cry for me Argentina", jazzing it up with my own little touches. The bloke appeared to have gone. Instead, two teenage girls in too-tight clothes and trowelled-on make-up stopped. Talking all the time they were. About me I think. Falling about, nudging each other, giggling. Maybe they could tell I was like an emaciated sparrow underneath the coat. Or maybe it was the purple socks and sandals in mid-winter. Not my fault my shoes had fallen apart, I thought. The girls' giggling was getting on my nerves. I stopped playing, put my violin down, crossed my arms and glared at them till they went silent and tottered off. No respect some people.

Twelve pounds, two dollars, a hundred lire, three old tube tickets, an old ticket for "Les Mis", a plastic Teenage Ninja Turtle, two buttons and various bits of fluff later, I began to pack up. It was time to make my way over to South Ken. Yesterday I'd got twenty five quid in my two hours here. And when Sonia and I were still busking together, we'd make much more. Yep, we used to make a packet.

I liked to have a laugh with the guards. Jim, he's always walking past with his fingers in his ears, his face screwed up like he's really in pain 'cause he can't stand the music. Other times he'll sing along, but *really* out of tune just to wind me up. 'Bugger off, Jim, I'm trying to earn a living,' I'd say. And Kabir would bring us delicious samosas made by his missis.

After picking out the junk and debris, I tipped the change into my pocket. Then, carefully, I put my violin in the case, together with the chinrest, and the bow alongside. As I was closing the case, fiddling with the catch (it's temperamental), I felt a tap on my shoulder. Blimey, I thought with a jump. The transport police. Instead, it was the bloke in the smart blue coat. He'd come back and was now grinning at me, like I was some long-lost friend.

I stood up. 'Do I know you, mate?' I said. I came up to his shoulder. Good haircut I thought-not like my D.I.Y. job.

'No, you don't know me,' he was grinning again and now pointing at my coat. 'But, well. I thought so earlier. And yes. You are. You're wearing my coat.'

'Sorry, mate,' I said. 'This is my coat.' Christ, I thought, why do I always get the loonies?

'D'you mind ...' he leaned forward. I thought he was making a lunge for me so I backed away, pressing myself against the "Hello Boys" ad. Then I realised that I'd got it all wrong. He was having a closer look at the coat. Was peering at it round about my chest, in fact.

'Yes, yes. See? It is my coat!' he said, pointing once more. 'See? The top button. It's sewn with dark green cotton because I'd run out of black!' And now he was waving this book about as he spoke. *Archy and Mehitabel*, it was. Poems.

'Look,' I said. 'If it means that much to you, you can have the coat back. No problem. It didn't cost much.' I don't know why I was prepared to give this geezer my coat. Spur of the moment thing, I guess. But I began to take it off.

'No, no,' he said laughing now. 'No need. I'd donated it to a charity shop anyway. Well, my girlfriend had. It was just funny spotting it today. It used to be my father's.' He shrugged his shoulders. 'Still, you can't hang on to all your old junk, can you?' And then his face clearly turned pink. Must be the sensitive type, I thought. Thinking of the poems and all.

'Sorry,' he continued. 'I didn't mean to say it's old junk. It's a pretty fine coat. Just that I bought this new coat, and my girlfriend ... well ...'

'It's okay, mate. Don't worry. It's a great coat. Just what I needed.' Then, because I was curious I asked: ' What's the book, then?'

'Oh. Poems about cats. Present for my girlfriend. She's mad about cats.' His expression said: W*omen eh? We have to indulge them.*

'Tell me about it,' I laughed, rather taking to this bloke. Nice to know that I got the coat from an all-right geezer. 'Bloody leave their filthy hairs all over the place. Don't they? I mean cats, not women.' The man laughed like I'd said the funniest thing he'd ever heard.

I smiled, thinking you haven't the first idea mate. My girlfriend, Sonia, she leaves her long blonde hairs *all over* the flat. Still, coincidence, nice chat or what, I didn't feel like spending any more time with my coat stalker. Things to do. Places to go. So after a brief conversation about the pros and cons of owning cats, I said I had to see a man about a dog and set off for South Kensington.

'By the way,' he added. 'Sorry, but I was distracted by the coat. What I really wanted to say was how much I enjoyed your playing.' I was about to thank him and walk off when he reached into his own coat. 'Here's my card,' he said, handing it to me. 'Give me a ring. I may have a job for you.'

'Cheers, mate,' I said. Not bothering to look at the card, cos you get all sorts of offers down here. 'Thanks, I will.' I started to walk off then called back over my shoulder. 'And don't worry about the coat, mate. I'll take good care of it.'

* * *

I changed at Victoria for South Ken. After a few hours underground you start to lose track of time. You come up expecting daylight only to find darkness and everyone gone. And you tend to guess at the weather by what people are wearing. Sometimes I don't feel part of the real world any more. I shivered and thought how I needed to see Sonia. Breathe her smell. I can't sleep without her next to me, I thought.

I looked at the card the coat stalker had given me. For some reason I hadn't thrown it away. *Deiter Davidson Burnet*, it said, *Cellist*. And a central London address. Well well well, I thought. That's a turn up for the books. And carefully stuffed it back in the inside pocket, then played some half-decent Mozart. The South Ken tunnel has brilliant acoustics. An old bloke in a crumpled raincoat with bright blue eyes stayed for half an hour. He left half a packet of Jaffa cakes. That's all. Stingy bastard, I thought, as I watched him walk away.

* * *

Two hours later, I was on the Piccadilly line eating the Jaffa cakes and reading The Beano (another donation) on my way home to Uxbridge. This bloke got on at Gloucester Road and sat opposite. He was covered in a layer of dust, and just briefly, I wondered about the possibility of a nuclear winter above ground.

Outside the tube station, I picked up a bottle of Chablis at the offie. The assistant had tutted as I counted out small change. Take away tonight, maybe, I thought, as I walked up the road. I'll tell Sonia about the coat stalker who may have a job for me, and the old man with the Jaffa cakes. And I'll tell her about the filth and the crowds and then she'll most likely tell me about "Les Mis", again. Only this time I won't make nasty remarks. I smiled to myself and was feeling dead cosy just thinking about her.

As I opened the door of our tiny flat, a cloud of steam with a hint of jasmine and undertones of cat hit me. She was in the bath with the door open. I hung up my coat, opened the wine, poured two glasses, and carried them into the bathroom. Sonia put her book down on the corner of the bath.

'Duggie,' she said, pulling her legs up to her chest. 'You're early.'

'Can I get in?' I said, pulling off my shirt and dropping it on the tiles.

'Listen Duggie, I…'

I went to kiss her, then caught sight of the cover of her book. *Archy and Mehitabel* by Don Marquis. I'd been going to tell her about the coat stalker. But seeing that book stopped me in my tracks.

'Duggie,' she was saying. 'I need to talk to you.' Her hair looked much darker when it was wet.

I needed to find something to say. Anything. 'How was the performance?' I said.

She started to say something when it crossed my mind that she might have *dyed* it. 'Have you dyed your hair, Son'?' I said.

'Yes, I've dyed my hair.' Her voice sounded weary, and she was staring at the taps instead of looking at me. 'I'm leaving you, Duggie,' was what she said next. 'I'm sorry.' Beads of condensation were on her face.

I guess I'd known that I was losing her – and that it was just a matter of time. And then the other realisation hit me. The coat. Of course. The bloody stupid coat. It had never seen the inside of a charity shop, had it?

I put my shirt back on–it was wet from the bathroom floor – then walked to the kitchen and sat down.

'Duggie?' I could hear splashing as she climbed out of the bath. 'Duggie …' she was saying. 'I'm sorry…..' She came in wearing only a towel. She'd never looked more beautiful.

'I love you, Sonia,' was all I could think to say. 'But if that's what you want, then I won't try and persuade you to stay.' She looked surprised. Relieved, even. 'Cos she knows what an awkward bastard I can be.

Instead I simply smiled back.

Katherine Wale

On My Mind

In bed with lover
counting Haiku syllables
on his shoulder blade.

School Pick-up Time

Hooded figures push
buggies under washed grey skies
towards the school gates.

Kitchen Slave

She scrapes potatoes
to sounds of Radio 4
and baying children.

Jenny May Forsyth

Rain

When it rains in Tofino, the Pacific comes down like Niagara. As she picked her way through the sleeping forest of sun-bleached driftwood, she pictured herself tiptoeing through the grave of a child who loved the beach. There wasn't much left of her daughter now, except for bones and teeth. The rain had long since cleaned away the flesh, what flesh there was after so short a life.

It was another watercolour day, this one awash with bluey greys. She stared at the sooty smudge that was the horizon, but couldn't make out where the ocean ended and the sky began. It was just like her life's horizon – a blur at the end of her past and the beginning of her future. She saw before her a future shaped by her past, but which past: 'before' or 'after'? Life had been just fine before that conversation with Tom.

For hours that seemed like days that passed in seconds, she wandered the beach, littered with barnacle-encrusted debris, a playground for scuttling crabs; death and life intertwined, a partnership not undone by the other's demise. The sea came in and then it went out.

Now and then she stopped at the kiosk for coffee or a hot dog. She watched the other customers, huddled under gigantic umbrellas with steaming cups and breath. What heartaches did they harbour beneath the smiles and cheery words? She wondered if anyone in the happy crowd had a new lover with a secret past, a secret that, sooner or later, would become a weapon to inflict new wounds, splashing bleeding sienna, and ochre pus, on the painting of their life.

* * *

Tom had talked of time passing and wounds not healing that day in the cafe in Holborn the previous week. They always went to cafes and restaurants, never pubs or wine bars. Tom hadn't had a drink in three years.

'I can't escape the guilt,' he said. 'Because of me, someone lost their father.'

'This is one hell of a confession,' she had said. She sipped her coffee. It was hot. She didn't mind. 'I thought you were teetotal for health reasons. Now, after six months, I find out this. Why didn't you tell me sooner?'

'I was afraid I'd lose you, especially after you told me what happened to your daughter. You think drink-drivers are evil and deserve the death sentence. I thought I needed to prove to you that I was a nice guy. One who just made one stupid mistake.' His coffee remained untouched, pristine with its heart-shaped chocolate sprinkling on the top.

'Your mistake cost someone their life. Were you punished?' she said, looking into his face for the answer.

'I'm always being punished, by my own conscience. But, yes, I was punished by the law, if that's what you mean. I got a suspended sentence and a hefty fine.'

'I don't call that punishment.' She pushed her coffee cup away.

'I'm sorry. I'm sorry every day. I'm sorry for him. I'm sorry for his family. I'm sorry for you. And I'm sorry for me. That one night ruined my life.'

'One night ruined my life as well. That's something else we have in common, then. Do you expect me to pity you?'

'I don't expect anything. I'm hoping you will forgive.'

'I don't know if I can.'

He didn't take his eyes from her during their conversation. She looked around the room, at the other customers, some laughing, some serious. She wondered if anyone was watching them, trying to guess the nature of their conversation. What mood did she and Tom convey? She looked out the window at swirling slate-coloured clouds preparing to relieve themselves of some great load only to burden those below. She wished she'd brought her umbrella. She watched spilled coffee on the floor slowly move toward her, froth getting closer to her new shoes. She didn't move her feet.

Whenever she met his gaze she couldn't look at him for long. She was confused. Until that night she thought he was a wonderful man. Kind and sincere. Now he looked like a small boy. She knew he felt bad about his moment of madness, but she couldn't help him. She said she was going home to Canada to think things through.

'When will you come back?' he asked.

'When things become clear. When the clouds shift.'

'Will you come back to me?'

'I don't know.'

* * *

When it got dark, she walked into town. The streetlights gave an illusion of warmth. Yet no light shone on her dilemma. If she went back to Tom, was it the same as forgiving her child's killer? Could she perceive one, but not the other, as a man shamed, imprisoned by his guilty conscience, enduring a living death? Did she want to?

In the wet light she saw a man stumble from a bar, towards a car. She ran over to him.

'Wait,' she said. 'Please don't drive in such a state. You might kill someone.'

'Mind your own,' the man said and thrust his middle finger in the air. The car door slammed and she watched it snake and skid out of the car park onto the road.

It was still raining.

Nathalia Gjersoe

Clara

Clara scuffed her feet along the pavement and hugged close to the wall to be as inconspicuous as possible. One hand worried the frayed ends of her belt whilst the other dragged absent-mindedly along the bricks. Every few minutes she peered up through her straggly fringe at the clock on the church then scowled at the hospital across the road. Was it time yet? Now? It must be time now! Yet she kept on pacing back and forth.

Surely there was no need for another one? The house was already a hurly-burly hive of noise and mess and fighting and giggles. Already they were sleeping two to a bed and, since Daddy had left to find his way, what were they to do? Clara had of course contemplated giving one of her siblings away. It seemed the decent thing to do after all, when she had so many and others, poor souls, had so few. But who would go? Patrick ate the most, but as the youngest had a sort of pride of place within the family and was frequently utilised as a plaything when other pastimes grew tedious. Besides, there was a certain sweetness in the way he guzzled, dimples waggling away as he chortled gleefully beneath his mask of gravy.

Then there was Samantha. Lovely Samantha who would beguile the neighbours and bring onlookers flocking as she floated gently down from the roof to the street below, petticoats billowing and ribbons a-flutter. Although she was the oldest she had grown so used to being treated like a simpleton that she had settled comfortably into the role. Though Clara had a debt of gratitude to Samantha for raising her so well whilst her parents had been busy, she had to consider the possibility that maybe it was Samantha that should go. It was such a bother, after all, having to constantly be prepared to stop whatever one was doing to hold her down when she had one of her little turns. Goodness, the one time Clara had forgotten, what hell there had been to pay! She'd only looked away for a second and off Samantha had gone, up into the stratosphere. It had been hours before they found her, perched uncomfortably in a yew tree and wrestling with a particularly nasty squirrel. The scandal! On the other hand, it had earned Clara quite a bit of kudos at school and it was only really a matter of time before Samantha was married off. Perhaps then they wouldn't have to wade through bouquets of sodden roses to get to the front door and keep the shutters closed day and night to ward off eager suitors. No, Samantha would just have to jolly well sit it out and hope for a beau who wasn't too bothered about a dowry. Clara had the growing suspicion that the secret collection of old handkerchiefs and toy camels she had been lovingly collecting for her sister's departure may not, in truth, be well received.

So that left Humphrey. He could definitely go. Fart-faced radish. Snaggle-toed rhinoceros. Snot-mottled grot-bag. She wouldn't mind terribly at all if she had to hand *him* over for the greater good. What with his swaggering and his "I'm the man of the family now" and his bossing about and refusing to be bossed and what-not. Full of his own importance, he was, rather too full for a ten year old. So full it was a wonder that it wasn't him that billowed away into the cosmos, fuelled by his own hot air. But as nicely as she had tried to suggest it to him, and as much as she explained the relative advantages, he selfishly and dogmatically refused to leave. She had attempted to sweeten the deal with bribes of gobstoppers and sherbet, but to no avail. Even careful subterfuge – trails of cake crumbs out the door, ghoulish noises from the cupboards and surreptitious packing of all his things – had failed to have any effect. Despairing, she had finally taken it upon herself to build him a very fine house from mud and leaves and sticks down the end of the garden. Within close proximity of all the local amenities, a fine view and open-plan design, it was everything any young bachelor could hope for. And yet, he *still* refused to budge.

And now another one on the way. Really! What was her mother thinking? And where on earth had it come from anyway? Her father had been gone for a year and, although her knowledge of the finer details of procreation were fuzzy, she was pretty sure there

80

definitely needed to be a man involved at some point during the process. She rubbed her knuckles slightly harder against the bricks in consternation. Right, that was it, she was going in and she was just going to have to like it or lump it, whatever it was.

Clara shook herself off, straightened her dress and sauntered across the road with a very business-like air about her despite the broken shoes and dress that was ever so slightly too short. Embarrassingly, she had to wait for someone slightly bigger to arrive before the electric doors would open but she held her composure admirably and conscientiously ignored all those people who didn't try to stop her as she marched to find her mother's room.

The corridor was remarkably quiet and empty, fairly reverberating with silence. Not to be outdone, Clara clacked her shoes louder along the tiles and hummed herself a jolly little tune. So loud was she humming, in fact, and with such concentration, that she almost stumbled over the nurse sitting outside her mother's door. The nurse's starched white uniform was slightly more creased now than it had been before and her knees were drawn up tightly under her chin as she rocked violently back and forth, teeth chattering and eyes glazed. Clara stopped in surprise and gazed at her a moment before tut-tutting at such deplorable lack of professionalism and carrying on her way.

On the cusp of meeting her new little brother or sister she steadied herself and prepared to be both courteous and welcoming. It wouldn't do at all to launch immediately into what an imposition the sudden arrival was nor how ill-prepared the family was to receive new members at this time. All that would have to wait. She pushed the door open to announce herself, beaming smile at the ready. There was a thud. And a small groan. She leaned her shoulder against the door and heaved with all her little might. It wouldn't budge another inch but with a lot of squirming and wriggling and grunting and squeezing she managed to scrape herself through.

It wasn't until she was standing, panting and slightly grazed on the other side, that she realised it was the prostrate body of her mother's doctor that had been impeding her progress. He groaned again as she stared at him and he feebly fluttered the fingers on his left hand which appeared to be bleeding from some sort of bite marks. Careful not to slip in the little puddle of blood she turned to greet her mother.

Willie Hewes

Bare Feet

She
A pair of boots in the waterline.
Side by side, so precisely, yet so abandoned.
The sun bravely penetrated the clouds, the sharp shells would
hurt
      bare feet.
There would be no hot tea with milk when I came home.

The round, brown laces tucked inside
      so precisely, so precise
Calm down, the gulls screeched, it's just a pair of boots
But who would leave the beach on bare feet?
Or who swam out to sea – on bare feet – never meaning to
return?

This was not a day at the beach
The rushing of waves was soothing, once.
The waves, they lied to me that day,
These boots, the rough brown sand and still
Clinging to the noses, sand,
      They were just like mine —

Why did she take off her boots, I wondered.
I looked at the sea
The horizon stretching from ear to ear
Such a perfect line, and yet so vague

Why did she take off her shoes?
She?
The boots asked me. The gulls laughed.
She? She?

Hiking boots, drenched with sea water and heavy
Why brave the broken shells on naked feet?

Jane Reece

Sorry Silence

Repentent eyes say
You wish you had not told me
All of your secrets.

Guy Fawkes Night

Against the night sky
We write our names in sparklers
They vanish quickly

Rosemary Dun

Raindrops On Roses

Her friend nudged her in the ribs: 'Psst. Take a look at that fit nun over there.'

'Where?'

'Next to the brown paper package.'

Mary craned her neck – trying to look without being spotted – and sure enough, there was the brown paper package complete with string. He winked at her. She blushed and sat back, but not before clocking the nun in question.

'Climb every mountain,' sang the Contessa – badly. Mary winced as the combined *Sing-along-a-Sound-of-Music* audience tried but failed to reach the top note.

'Christ Almighty,' whispered the Contessa as she smoothed her emerald-encrusted dress. 'That was high. I nearly ruptured myself.'

'Ssh,' scolded Mary, wishing she'd come in lederhosen or something sexy. Instead, Kate the Contessa had insisted that Mary don the full Julie Andrews attire. And what could she do? Kate *was* paying for it.

'My treat,' she'd said last month after talking Mary into accompanying her to the Singalong at Brighton's Theatre Royal.

'How come you get to be the Contessa?'

'Dahlink, to sink I could be anybody else.'

And it was true. There was an impervious air about tall, dark, Kate which made her formidable at meetings, yet had young men slavering over her whenever she went on the prowl along Brighton's beachside clubs and bars.

They'd met at work, in London, when they were both in their early twenties. Early on, they'd discovered a shared trait.

'Blimey, my knees are burning. I must be pisshed. I get hot knees when I'm pisshed.'

'No! Me too!'

And the bond was formed. An appropriate one too, as they'd

86

sealed their friendship around drinking, parties, meals out. It was Mary who had first moved to Brighton – her friend following a couple of years later.

During the show's interval, Kate wasted no time in making further contact with the 'man with the habit' – as Mary now referred to him in her head. The theatre bar thronged with an assortment of Nazis, Austrian counts and contessas, nuns, Von Trapps, raindrops on roses – you get the picture.

'So, are you a flibberty jibbet?'

'A willow the wisp?'

'A clown? Honk honk!'

Demanded three snowflakes, as they fluttered about Mary.

'Push off,' snarled a kitten, all curves in black PVC catsuit. 'Hey babe,' she purred, as the three snowflakes flounced off. 'Mm. Haven't I seen you in Pussy Galore?'

The kitty was definitely coming on to Mary, so she sidled over to stand by Kate, hoping that would field any messy need for a brush off.

Kate merely said 'Oh,' then 'Hi,' rather begrudgingly when Mary joined her and her nun. Kate did not seem best pleased. Her nun had his headdress wimple thing off and now Mary could see he was the waiter from last night's pizzeria. Kate had her arm draped over his shoulder. She smiled pointedly at Mary, who didn't need Mystic Meg to tell her that she'd be getting a taxi home on her own tonight – again.

Three bells sounded their call for the start of the second half. She turned to Kate: 'You coming?'

'Yeah, yeah. In a minute. You go on ahead.'

Mary gave her a look.

'I'll be there, I promise. I haven't forgotten.'

Because the last time Kate had done this Mary told her how pissed off it made her – being stranded the moment some likely man came along. 'Your friends should mean more to you than that,' she'd told her. Ah, what's the use, she thought, as she returned, alone, to her theatre seat.

Half an hour later, Julie Andrews was skipping through alpine meadows with the Von Trapp children, all clad in clothes made from curtains. As they began their *Do Ray Mi* song, Mary was all too aware of the empty seat next to her, and of Kate's broken promise.

'Meow,' tantalized the kitten who was sat behind, from where she proceeded to try and stroke Mary's wavy hair with her long fake fur tail.

'Gerroff!'

That's it, thought Mary. I've had enough. She got up and walked out, muttering Bloody Kate, under her breath. Outside, she breathed in the night air, sharp as a chilled glass of water, then set off for the taxi rank. And, with no particular thought or purpose in mind, happened to glance sideways down the alley next to the theatre where she could see, just out of range of the street light, a billowing and a flapping of voluminous black nun skirt and sparkly green ball gown. The nun was clearly breaking his vow of celibacy up against the wall with a dishevelled Contessa. They didn't spot Mary.

'Don't mind me,' she muttered loud enough for them to hear. But they didn't. Overhead, a pigeon who'd been trying to get some kip, huffed out its feathers and gazed down at her. She almost said, 'sorry,' to the pigeon, but instead collided with a roller blader.

'Ooof!'

The man was on his feet first. Looks too ancient to be roller blading, thought Mary, who had banged her head.

'Here, let me help you up,' said the elderly man giving her the benefit of his warm and sparkly smile. It was particularly sparkly as he was wearing a pink tutu complete with tiara and wand.

'Thanks.' She dusted down her own full Julie Andrews/ Maria type skirt, then peered at him. 'Are you supposed to be a snowflake?'

He didn't answer, but instead sprinkled her with fairy dust. Which is definitely surreal, she thought. She wondered if she was having an *Ally McBeal* moment and whether or not that meant she could expect Al Green or Gladys Knight and The Pips to suddenly appear and burst into song. She stood still, and listened. Don't be silly. This is a *Sound of Music* night, not *Soul Train*.

She touched her forehead, and suspected that tomorrow her sore patch would transform into a sizeable lump.

The fairy godfather, guardian angel, or whoever he was, said: 'You know, we only make friends with people who can teach us a lesson.' He waved some more fairy dust. 'One can't help observing that a true friend wouldn't have deserted you like that.' A posh fairy, then, thought Mary.

'Oh, that's just Kate. I'm used to her going off with some bloke,' she said, clearly not. 'Anyway, a friend in need is a pain in the neck, is what Kate says.'

He merely smiled his twinkly smile at her.

'Just a minute.' She peered harder at the man. 'How do you know all this anyway? You some kind of stalker?'

He tapped his nose - *'Raindrops on roses and bright woollen mittens …'* he sang; and was off. What's more, he appears to have vanished into thin air. She rubbed her head. Either that, or I've got concussion.

Two flights up on its stone window ledge, the pigeon moved its wings in a gesture which very closely resembled a shrug, then turned its back.

* * *

Next morning, Mary was sat outdoors, at her favourite café on the seaside prom, from where she was enjoying a large mug of tea, a rock cake, and a toasted bacon sandwich. Even though she didn't have the hangover she'd planned to have – due to her abandonment by Kate – she was blowed if she wasn't going to have her hangover cure anyway. And it might help her aching head too.

She breathed deep of the salt air. Brighton, she loved it. She loved to sit here and watch the unmarried mums parading love bites as they pushed buggies full to bursting with screaming kids garbed in *Osh Gosh* dungarees. They mingled along the prom with celebrities and new Regency fops dressed in their chi chi finery. These were the *beacherati*, as she liked to call them, who flocked to see and be seen every sunny weekend, as Brighton did its Sunday promenade. Never mind London by the Sea, she thought, its getting more and more like *Sex And The City* by the Sea.

Even so, she thought – sitting sat back in her chair and taking another deep and restorative breath of sea air – I do love it. And I love the way that on days like this, it isn't in the least bit unusual to see a pensioner gliding along on a silver micro scooter. Just like this one. Dressed in his pink fairy tutu and a matching fluffy pink cardigan ... She sat up. What the ...?

'Did you find your friend?' he called out, as he glided past.

'No, I ...' and he was off. Again.

Mary stared after him as he disappeared down the walkway. He was starting to get on her nerves, she decided, rubbing her still throbbing temple. Because, ok, she knew Brighton was a small town where anything could and probably would happen – and that quite frankly you have to expect the unexpected – but really ... She did hope that his fairy interruptions were a passing phase. I mean, pink angels, fairy godfathers, or whatevers, are pretty unsettling at night. Let alone during the day ...?

'Hi, honey!' helloed Kate as she spotted her then headed down for café, her long strides taking her past the stone angel statue which guards the spot where Brighton ends and Hove begins. The spot where *The Meeting Place* café sits, bordering Brighton and Hove's shingle beach.

'Thought I'd find you here.'

'Yes, here I am,' said Mary, rather grumpily. She wasn't sure she was in the mood for Kate.

Kate plonked a kiss on her cheek, then flopped in the seat opposite. As if last night never happened, noticed Mary, who remained out of sorts. Her headache didn't help.

'Who was that old geezer, then? He your sugar daddy?'

'More like my sugar plum fairy,' murmured Mary, then smiled as she thought: That's good, that is. Sugar plum fairy.

'What? What are you smiling at?'

'Oh nothing, really,' said Mary, not yet ready to be drawn into a relaxed conversation with Kate. She wasn't going to let her off the hook that easily. Then she gave in a little and added: 'Just thought he might have been my guardian angel or something for a moment there.'

'You what?'

'Exactly. Must have been having a mystical moment, I guess – if that makes sense,' she glanced at Kate's blank face, '… apparently not.'

'That's Brighton for you,' said her friend, all bright and breezy. 'You're so funny, babe. Look, I fancy a cuppa. You want anything?' she asked, beginning to get up. 'Although,' as she surveyed the debris of cake, bacon butty and tea in front of Mary, 'seems like you've had yours.'

She hasn't even noticed that I'm cheesed off. 'Get me another cup of tea, then,' she said.

Kate strode off to the counter, collecting several admiring glances from various men sat with their late breakfast pick-me-ups on the tables in front of them. Mary watched her go. She had to admit, that even the morning after, Kate looked magnificent. She was wearing one of those ethnic dresses from their favourite shop in North Laine. Her elegant legs glimpsed more fully as the opening, afforded by its cross-over tie front, flapped in the breeze. Mary could see the attraction. If she was a bloke she'd fancy Kate herself.

Kate returned, placed the cups on the round metal café table, then pulled out a large pair of white framed sunglasses. She gave Mary a broad beam.

'Sorry about last night,' she said. 'But he was well fit.'

Mary wasn't quite ready to forgive her old chum. She was miffed – but there again … She regarded her friend. 'OK. Go on then,' she relented. 'How did it go with pizza man?'

'The wimple with the pimples?' said Kate, stretching her legs out in front of her, and crossing them at the ankles.

'Yeah, well. He was a bit young – even for you,' said Mary as she finished the remains of her bacon butty.

'Oooo. I'll ignore that. I'll say this for him, he certainly kept to Perfect Pizza's promise of delivery within half an hour.'

Mary chortled. 'You old slapper!' She couldn't deny that Kate was a laugh.

A pigeon, about to alight on their table, changed its mind and crashlanded near her foot, from where it proceeded to pretend that that was what it had meant to do all along.

'Dahlink, an old slapper is just about what he called me. The nerve.'

'No!'

'Yep,' she reached forward to pinch a piece of Mary's rock cake which she'd been saving to have with her cup of tea. "And after I'd given him the benefit of my contessa–charms,' she added, licking her fingertips. 'Afraid he had to go.'

The pigeon edged nearer.

'Go?'

'Of course. Cheeky begger. Oh, and speaking of going,' she added. 'Where on earth did you disappear to last night?' She gave Mary a conciliatory smile. 'I'm a cow, I know. And I really am sorry, babe. I did come back for you, honest. And I couldn't have been gone for ever so long. But when I returned, you'd already left – without me.'

'Yeah, well.'

'Oh god,' Kate carried on as she leant forwards to touch Mary's hand. 'I didn't tell you, did I?'

'What?'

She laughed. 'You'll never guess what happened after I'd had my portion of pepperoni.'

'Puh-lease!'

'No, no, you'll love this! I ended up having to floor a rather persistent pvc-clad kitty kat. Fur flying – the whole lot.' Mary and the pigeon gave her a look. 'Talk about not taking no for an answer!'

Mary laughed, remembering her own run–in with the kat in the back. She watched as Kate moved her feet, causing the pigeon, who was about to spear a crumb with its tattered beak, to creakily unfurl its scruffy feathers and fly off. Mary rubbed the bump on her head. She could have sworn that pigeon winked at her.

'By the way,' added Kate. 'Remind me never to set foot in Pussy Galore again.'

Mary was now wholeheartedly laughing at the spectacle she'd missed as Kate gave her a blow-by-blow account. Kate and kitty kat, fighting. Hilarious.

'What are you like?'

Kate leant over to give her a hug. 'Forgive me,' she said. 'Go on. You know you want to. Please. Pretty please. I have improved – this time I didn't totally leave you, now did I? Eh?'

Mary sat back in her plastic chair, mulling over last night and Kate's escapades. OK, Kate can be a pain, but, you know what? she thought, smiling to herself. Never mind raindrops on roses. Kate is one of my top favourite things.

'What?' said Kate. 'What'

But Mary was on her feet, pulling her friend out of her chair. 'Come on,' she laughed. 'Race you to the sea! Last one there buys lunch!'

And as they ran, the wind rushing past her ears sounded very much like The Sound of Music.

Notes on the authors

Jenny May Forsyth has been writing short stories on and off since she was very young and is currently tackling her first novel. Her inspiration comes from her childhood in Vancouver. She is married, mid-40s and now lives in Bristol following a couple of decades working in London's media industry

Jane Reece is a writer/researcher/teacher with a MA in Creative Writing (University of Sussex). She is fascinated at how writing creatively allows us to explore new possibilities within our lives. She writes best in the early morning or very late at night.

Nathalia Gjersoe grew up in Papua New Guinea with 5 crocodiles and 3 goats andspent most of her time under water. She's now doing a PhD on how children perceive magic. She's particularly fond of butternut squash and ice-cream, but not together. She owns more condiments than is generally considered normal.

Alex Maxwell is 38 and juggles being mother of two, part-time career and house wife stuff with scribbling short stories. This will be the first time she has been published - hoorah!

Tamar Zak is currently working on her first novel, American coming of age story, *Three*. She holds a distinction in Creative Writing from the MA programme at Cardiff University and is a short story writer. Her work is primarily centred around the exploration of contemporary gay issues and often draws influence from her native San Francisco. She is a musician as well as a writer, and sings and plays guitar in indie-folk duo, dayriser.

Paul Roberts. Around the time of his 30th birthday, having just returned from an enforced extension to an Himalayan adventure, Paul decided it was time to bring more to his life than the humdrum sex, drugs and rock and roll. So he started writing, and joined the classes at the Folk House.

Cathy Wilson. Born in Yorkshire, Cathy meandered steadily southward, arriving in Bristol in 1987. After years of secret scribbling, she joined her first writing class at the Folk House, in time for the new Millennium. Now active in several local poetry groups, she is working towards the Diploma in Creative Writing at Bristol University.

Caroline Ward has lived in Bristol since 1971. Since then she has written some poetry, made thousands of loaves of bread and enjoyed countless library books. Both her jobs contain elements of the unexpected. She is not a passionate team player

Tighe O'Connor lives in Frome. He's not sure how he ended up there but is glad he has. He came to writing recently following careers in football, music and mathematics….it was a deliberate lateness. His debut novel 'Peoplewatching' has now been completed. He is unreasonably obsessed with the number 12.

Ginetta Martinez lives in Bristol.

Judy Green taught writing in primary schools for many years but has recently taken courses at the Folk House to develop her own work. She prefers writing poetry and generally uses humour in her observations about the world. Her work has been published in the Evening Post and Venue magazine.

Roy Hilliar. Born a war baby, fostered and adopted, Roy was never encouraged to talk or express his emotions. He hated school as his verbal and written communication skills were poor. Now, at the age of 68 years, through writing poetry, he has found a way of expressing his emotions and his love of nature.

Willie Hewes is a writing and drawing girl-person living in Bristol. By day, she works in the service of Lord Blair, ruler of Great Britain, but by night, she turns into a pen-wielding superhero of tragic fantasy and romance. Much of her work can be found online, at www.williehewes.co.uk.

Dinah Foweraker. Born and brought up in Bristol, Dinah studied English Literature at university, which had the unintended consequence of inhibiting her own attempts to write fiction. In 2001 she started attending short story classes at the Folk House, and has since managed to write a number of short stories and experimental pieces.

Paul Hilton finds time in between his day job to craft stories that he shows off to a lazy group of writers. Pot addled and pretentious, Paul writes music reviews for a magazine that could be a figment of someone's imagination. He currently lives in a Clifton bubble with his partner.

Katharine Wale joined a Bristol writers group about a year ago, after being re-inspired by a couple of creative writing courses at the Folk House. Her main interest is writing short stories (she never thought she'd ever write poetry again after leaving school...). She finds the whole writing process painfully slow, but exhilarating. She is addicted!

Sarah O'Neill is a secretary, cabaret organiser and frequent traveller, who dabbles in writing for pleasure with sporadic regularity. She is presently reading 'The Sea, The Sea' by Iris Murdoch. She loves festivals, sunshine, treehouses and owns a tipi. She dreams of a self–sufficient lifestyle in the sun.

Clare Harris was born in 1964 and grew up in Norfolk. She has lived in Bristol since 1991 and works here as a psychotherapist. Her daughter was born last year. These are her first published poems

Ross Rossiter grew up on one of the roughest estates in a Somerset village called Evercreech. He now lives and works in Bristol.

Kate Gardiner has taught creative writing to adults at Bristol Folk House since completing her MA in 2000. She has also mentored students at Cardiff University and worked with secondary school pupils. Her poetry has been published in the New Welsh Review. Multi-talented Kate not only writes and tutors, but is also a textile artist www.kategardiner.co.uk

Rosemary Dun has managed to turn her hobby of staring out the window and drinking cups of coffee, plus occasionally showing off, into a career. She now writes, teaches creative writing and performance poetry. She has a MA in Creative Writing, performs poetry and puts on spoken word and music events under the colourful parasol of Big Mouth Poetry. www.rosemarydun.co.uk, www.big-mouth-poetry.